Go to Joseph

BY FR. RICHARD W. GILSDORF
EDITED BY PATRICK F. BENO

STAR OF THE BAY PRESS

Copyright © 2009 Star of the Bay Press

Published by Star of the Bay Press
2345 Sunrise Court
Green Bay, Wisconsin 54302
www.esto-vir.org
www.CatholicWord.com

Nihil obstat: Very Rev. John F. Doerfler, STD, JCL
Imprimatur: Most Rev. David L. Ricken, DD, JCL, bishop of
the Diocese of Green Bay

The Scripture verses herein primarily come from the
Confraternity of Christian Doctrine version, 1941. When the
wording seemed more suited to the subject, the editors used
either the Douai-Rheims version or the Revised Standard
Version-Catholic Edition.

Library of Congress Control Number: 2009926337

Editors: Patrick Beno, Sr., Brian O'Neel

Interior layout: Mike Fontecchio
Cover design: Ted Schluenderfritz, Five Sparrows Media
(www.5sparrows.com)

Printed in the United States of America by Worzalla
Publishing Co., Stevens Point, WI.

ISBN 978-0-692-00300-8

CONTENTS

TESTIMONIALS

This is a fascinating—and rather charming—book on St. Joseph with many insights into aspects of his life and its message that will be new to readers. St. Joseph is apt to be an almost cliché figure for Catholics, someone who scarcely seems real because he is so familiar. But he was a real person who played a central role in the most dramatic and important event of all human history—the Incarnation. This new book tells the story in a way that makes it seem fresh and thrilling and allows you to walk alongside St. Joseph through the events that brought us salvation. With the saint, you are alongside Christ, the Son of God, as a baby in Bethlehem, a little boy at Nazareth, a young man busy at work, and in the family home. If you have felt that the Christian story seems remote or bleak, this book offers you a change of perspective. Read it and relish it.

~ Joanna Bogle
EWTN personality and author

For those who already know and love St. Joseph, this book will be a delight; for those who do not, this book will be a welcome discovery. Fr. Gilsdorf has done us a great service in promoting devotion to St. Joseph, Master of the Interior Life. Drawing upon the Fathers and other saints and scholars, Fr. Gilsdorf has brought to light the remarkable life of the greatest husband and father who ever lived. In an age when men need a model of masculine fidelity, St. Joseph proves to be an inspiring example.

> ~ Fr. Francis Joseph Hoffman, JCD
> Chaplain of Northridge Prep and
> Relevant Radio host

St. Joseph stands alone in history as a model for men. He is husband, father, worker, provider, planner, doer, and man of prayer. This book, grounded in history and Tradition, brings him into sharp focus. We see him as he is, and with Fr. Gilsdorf's good guidance we can follow where he has gone before us.

> ~ Mike Aquilina
> EWTN host and author of
> *The Fathers of the Church*

DEDICATIONS

Dedicated to the memory of
Fr. Francis L. Filas, SJ,
scholarly apostle and zealous promoter
of devotion to St. Joseph

Editor's additional dedications:

To the respected Josephs in my life:

John Joseph Beno—my father (deceased)
Joseph Jagers—my father-in-law (deceased)
Joseph Gouin—my grandson
Joseph Ellis—my godson
Joseph Cardinal Ratzinger (Pope Benedict XVI)

Finally, to Fr. Tony Dolski, a priest since Saturday, May 23, 1959, who served at St. Joseph Church in Green Bay from 1962-1986. He has been a close friend of mine and was also very dear to Fr. Gilsdorf. He has given excellent advice, direction, and comfort both on this book and *The Signs of the Times: Understanding the Church since Vatican II*, for which I am immeasurably grateful. May God always bless this great priest and all priests in this, the Year of the Priest.

Acknowledgments

In this author's opinion, Fr. Francis L. Filas, SJ, researched and wrote the most thorough scholarly works on St. Joseph, and he devoted 15 years to this labor of love. (Filas also served with distinction as chairman of the Theology Department at Loyola University, Chicago.)[i] As

---

[i] Fr. Filas was born in Cicero, IL, on June 4, 1915. After discerning his vocation as a young altar boy, he entered the Jesuits in 1932, took his first vows in 1934, and received Holy Orders in June 1945.

During his career, he wrote extensively on Our Lord's earthly father, his first book being 1944's *The Man Nearest to Christ*, which dealt with the nature and history of the devotion to St. Joseph. It sold out in two weeks.

His next book was *The Family for Families*, which considered how the Holy Family is the model for all families and which saw at least six printings.

Having taught high school during World War II, he joined the theology faculty at the University of Detroit following the war. During this time, he was involved in the then-new ministry to married couples, at the time known as the Cana Conference. His superiors moved him to Loyola in 1950.

His next book on St. Joseph grew out of his doctoral dissertation and was titled, *Joseph and Jesus: A theological study of their relationship*. He followed this with the 1957 work, *Joseph Most Just: The logical questions about St. Joseph*.

such, this booklet relies on some of the historical data Fr. Filas presented and uses the extensive patristic and papal documents he cited in his works. Some of these may be translations from the original by Fr. Filas.

The author wrote the first words of this booklet on Christmas Eve.[ii] The final words were written on March 19, the feast of St. Joseph.

Editor's additional acknowledgments:

A special thanks to Shirley Farrell, for her assistance in preparing the manuscript, and to Ann Shibler, Mike Hahn, Valerie Pokorny, and Kate Vrazel for their excellent proofreading work.

One of the world's foremost researchers on the Shroud of Turin, the reputed burial shroud of Jesus Christ, he determined that an imprint of a coin on the cloth matched similar coins produced between 29–32 AD in Judea during the reign of Pontius Pilate. He died February 15, 1985, after a 35-year association with Loyola.

[ii] It is believed the Christmas Eve referred to here was 1988. Father's health problems began shortly after he completed this manuscript, and he was never able to give it the subsequent attention it deserved.

SOURCES

In this small book, it is our intention to rely on the witness of Scripture as our primary and surest guide. We will also delve into the great "mystery of silence" concerning Joseph in Scripture and its divinely intended purpose. Of course, this silence affects not only Joseph but Mary, as well (albeit to a lesser degree).

However, while we first need to consider Scripture, no account of Joseph's life can fail to consider other sources. This is partly because Scripture's reticence to give more than the essential facts has led Christians to embellish what details do exist. Primary among these embellishments are six major early works, referred to as the apocrypha (from the Greek word for "hidden information"), the most influential among these being the so-called "Proto-Gospel of James."

There may be some nuggets of historical fact in these sources, but the main reason for mentioning these accounts is that they are responsible for some serious errors that have come down to us through the centuries.

For example, we cannot take as "gospel truth" the accounts of Joseph's betrothal to Mary where the high priest supposedly designated him on the basis of his walking stick, which, depending on the account, either produced a dove or blossomed. If we think about it, even less acceptable is the picture of Joseph as old, even decrepit, having had an earlier marriage and numerous children. (We will examine these enduring legends as we continue our study.)

Of course, some extra biblical sources deserve much more respect since they are private revelations given to unquestionably holy souls. Of particular note among these are *The Mystical City of God* by Ven. Mary of Ágreda[iii] and *The Life of the Blessed Virgin Mary* by Bl. Anne Catherine Emmerich.[iv]

[iii] Mary (1602–1665) was an abbess in the town of Ágreda, Spain. The product of a noble family, her father and brothers entered a monastery, while she, her mother, and sister founded a Franciscan nunnery. While she is reputed to have had the powers of bilocation (a power granted to certain saints to be in two places at once), she is best known for her mystical writings on the life of Christ and His mother. She is buried in the Monastery of La Concepción in Ágreda, where her body, most recently examined in 1989, is still perfectly incorrupt.

[iv] Anne Catherine Emmerich (1774–1824) was a Roman Catholic Augustinian nun, stigmatic, mystic, visionary, and ecstatic whose visions were transcribed by the famous poet

For instance, the latter, a stigmatist nun, recounts the day-by-day life of Christ as shown to her in visions. These display an uncanny acquaintance with the history, customs, geography, and place names of the times, as well as the subtleties of Aramaic.

Of course, when we consider the mystics, we must always keep in mind the disclaimer made by Clemens Brentano in his preface to the first edition of Anne Catherine Emmerich's *The Dolorous Passion of Our Lord Jesus Christ*. He states:

> Though the accounts of these visions may appear in some degree remarkable among many similar fruits of the contemplative love of Jesus, they solemnly reject the slightest claim to bear the character of historical truth. All that they wish to do is to associate themselves with the countless representations of the Passion by artists and pious writers and to be regarded as a pious nun's Lenten meditations imperfectly comprehended and narrated and also very clumsily set down. She never attached to her visions anything more than a human and defective value, and therefore yielded to an inner admonition to

---

Clemens Brentano. It was her visions that led researchers to discover the house of Our Lady at Ephesus after 1,800 years.

communicate to them only in obedience
to the repeated commands of her spiritual
directors and after a hard struggle with
herself.

Citing this, the preface to the German
edition of *The Life of the Blessed Virgin Mary*
adds:

> The same applies in essentials to the *Life
> of Mary* here presented.... However the
> historical or theological character of the
> work may be judged, it is acknowledged to
> be a treasury of holy scenes and pictures that
> contribute to the edification and inspiration
> of the faithful.

EDITOR'S PREFACE

In the process of compiling the papers of Fr.
Richard Gilsdorf for the book *The Signs of the
Times: Understanding the Church since Vatican II*,
I discovered a partially completed manuscript
entitled *Go to Joseph*.

At the time, I decided to set it aside because
I felt it too long to include in the book that was
eventually published. The national and partly
international acceptance of *The Signs of the Times*
exceeded my wildest expectations. With the first
and second printing having sold out, and with
5,000 copies now in print (and sales still moving
briskly), I thought it an opportune time to
reexamine Father's study of St. Joseph. Indeed,
it is a worthy endeavor in its own right.

From the many conversations I had with
Fr. Gilsdorf, I sensed a very deep devotion
to the person of St. Joseph. He probably had
this instilled early in his life when he attended
school as a young boy at St. Joseph Church on
the west side of Green Bay, Wisconsin. His
parents lived only two blocks from the school

and the church. At St. Joseph's, he received baptism, his first confession, first Communion, and confirmation, and he loyally served at the altar during Mass. This parish is also where the love of Jesus, Mary, and Joseph became a very important part of his devotional life.

In turn, Father had the seeds of his vocation slowly nurtured at St. Joseph's, as well as in the confines of his devout Catholic family. Additionally, it was at St. Joseph's where he celebrated his first Holy Sacrifice of the Mass after his priestly ordination for the Diocese of Green Bay.

During the pastorate of Fr. Arthur Danks and his associate pastor Fr. Tony Dolski at St. Joseph's, during the 1970s, '80s, and '90s, these friends of Fr. Gilsdorf's called on him time and again to present his famous Scripture classes, which were attended by hundreds of parishioners and visitors. He never turned down an invitation to help out, especially during Lent, even though he had his own parish. He loved that parish's Catholic atmosphere because, I am sure, he recognized the influence and intercession of St. Joseph on its work and on all the people there.

The book you hold in your hands, therefore, is a testimony to Fr. Gilsdorf's deep devotion and an example of the unceasing labors of a priest who loved his vocation and continually bent himself to the task of ongoing formation and learning.

As a result, you have the opportunity to entertain and meditate upon the fruits of this formation and learning, these exceptional insights into the life of St. Joseph, arguably the Church's greatest male saint.

One final note: While solely drawing upon wholly faithful, traditional, and orthodox sources, Father nonetheless challenges many of the pious beliefs about St. Joseph that many understandably cherish. If the reader desires to hold fast to his or her beliefs on this or that account, that is fine. The areas Father challenges, after all, are not matters of divine revelation but private revelation. Thus the Church lets us accept or reject these where she has not made some final deliberation to the contrary.

These meditations, therefore, are simply meant to help stimulate the reflections of the faithful and thus help them grow closer to God. I don't doubt that they will.

Please enjoy.

> ～ Patrick F. Beno
> Editor

FOREWORD

St. Joseph is the patron of the Universal Church, yet relatively little has been written about this great saint. This is why I am so grateful for this short book, *Go to Joseph*, by Fr. Richard Gilsdorf.

Fr. Gilsdorf, a priest of the Diocese of Green Bay, died a few years before I was installed as the bishop of this diocese. I regret that I did not have the opportunity to meet him in person, though I have come to know his dedication to the priesthood through this book. He writes this book as a pastor, hoping that the readers will come to a deeper union with God, through devotion to St. Joseph and in communion with the Church.

Father's erudition as a Scripture scholar is also evident. He brings a depth of understanding of sacred Scripture to his reflections on the life of St. Joseph. Yet, he writes in a fashion that is accessible to the reader, bringing to light how much is contained in the few passages relating to this great saint. Father's approach to the life of St. Joseph, grounded in sacred Scripture, provides a sound basis for the devotion of the faithful. Devotion rooted in sacred Scripture and the teachings of the Church is ever rich and fruitful.

Devotion to St. Joseph strengthens families, sows vocations to holiness, strengthens our commitments to justice, and safeguards our relationship with Christ.

Fr. Gilsdorf has written a fine book on St. Joseph, and it is my hope that its publication will foster greater devotion to St. Joseph and holiness in the People of God.

~ Most Reverend David L. Ricken, DD, JCL
Bishop of Green Bay

CHAPTER ONE

THE MAN BY THE MANGER

I write these first words of this cherished task late on Christmas Eve. Soon, at Midnight Mass, we will once more retell—and renew—the tenderest mystery. All eyes will focus on the crib.

For the Christmas pageant, our first graders will play shepherds and, followed by two of their number chosen to represent Mary and Joseph, will escort the statue of the Infant and place Him in the manger.

After an inimitable "Silent Night," the children will have a few questions posed to them. Who is this Baby, and who is this beautiful lady? Who is that man standing beside the manger?

Our children will know that man quite well since he has been mentioned often during Advent, both in the classroom and from the pulpit. This may not be the case everywhere. He has often been neglected, and the importance of his sublime mission has been ignored. (Little

wonder in an age when even Mary's role has
been less than fully appreciated.)

The purpose of this little book, therefore,
is to concentrate on St. Joseph, the "just man,"
as St. Matthew calls him.[1] On this Christmas
night, the person and mission of Joseph come
into sharp focus.

The rest of these meditations will focus on
his role in relation to Mary and Jesus. In the
final analysis, the reader is encouraged to think
back to that mystic midnight by the crib and
consider how it all centers there.

Indeed, in light of this night, let us begin by
mentioning one aspect of Joseph's life.

First (as medieval theologians and modern
popes have well noted), Joseph fulfills the type
of that other Joseph,[i] the patriarch whose life is
so touchingly presented in the final chapters of
Genesis.

The first Joseph, the beloved favored son

---

[i] According to Fr. John Hardon's *Modern Catholic Dictionary*,
a biblical type is a "biblical person, thing, action, or event
that foreshadows new truths, new actions, or new events.
In the Old Testament, Melchizedech and Jonah are types
of Jesus Christ. A likeness must exist between the type
and the archetype, but the latter is always greater. Both
are independent of each other. God's call for the return of
the Israelites from Pharaoh's bondage typifies the return
of Jesus Christ from His flight into Egypt. In the New
Testament the destruction of Jerusalem, foretold by Christ,
was the antitype of the end of the world."

of Jacob, was forced to go into Egypt. He was guided by heavenly dreams that he interpreted with precision, and then Pharaoh summoned him to interpret his own perplexing dreams.

One of these foresaw seven years of plenty and seven years of famine. Joseph counseled the stockpiling and careful guarding of grain during the years of plenty for prudent, cautious distribution in the period of famine. Pharaoh trusted his interpretation, took his advice, and made Joseph "grand vizier," second only to himself in all Egypt. "He made him lord of his house and ruler of all his possessions."[2] The hungry were sent to Joseph with the words, "Go to Joseph! What he says to you, do."[3]

It is true that the early Church Fathers occasionally spoke of the first Joseph as a type of the second, but the first major comparison to this effect came from St. Bernard of Clairvaux.[ii] Since that time, the popes have built on this firm foundation.

Let us reflect on two passages as examples.

In a special decree titled *Quemadmodum Deus*, promulgated by the Sacred Congregation of Rites on behalf of Bl. Pius IX, the Pope

---

[ii] A Frenchman, St. Bernard (1090–1153) was the primary founder of the Cistercian order and a hugely influential man in the Church of his time. He was canonized a mere 21 years after his death, and declared a Doctor of the Church by Pius VIII in 1830.

declared Joseph "Patron of the Universal
Church." In this document, he refers to Joseph
of Egypt as a type of Joseph of Nazareth:

> As almighty God appointed Joseph, son of the
> patriarch Jacob, over all the land of Egypt to
> save grain for the people, so when the fullness
> of time was come and He was about to send
> to earth His only-begotten Son, the Savior
> of the world, He chose another Joseph, of
> whom the first had been the type, and He
> made him the lord and chief of His household
> and possessions, the guardian of His choicest
> treasures.... Him whom countless kings
> and prophets had desired to see, Joseph not
> only saw but conversed with, and embraced
> in paternal affection, and kissed. He most
> diligently reared Him whom the faithful
> were to receive as the bread that came down
> from heaven whereby they might obtain
> eternal life.[4]

In his encyclical of August 15, 1889,
Quamquam Pluries, Pope Leo XIII develops the
type:

> There was even a more evident similarity
> when by the [pharaoh's] order, [Joseph]
> was given supreme power over the entire
> kingdom. When calamity brought on a
> deficient harvest and a scarcity of grain, he

exercised such excellent foresight in behalf of the Egyptians and their neighbors that the [pharaoh] decreed he should be styled "savior of the world." Thus in that ancient patriarch we may recognize the distinct image of St. Joseph. As the first caused the prosperity of his master's domestic interests and at the same time rendered great services to the whole kingdom, so the second, destined to be the guardian of the Christian religion, should be regarded as the protector and defender of the Church, which is truly the house of the Lord and the kingdom of God on earth.[5]

In the atmosphere of Christmas, however, we can go beyond these statements to add some further details of comparison.

Keeping vigil over the Child, our Joseph is truly patriarch of a "new Genesis."[iii] Guided by dreams, Joseph stands beside Jesus, the new Adam, and Mary, the new Eve. As He Himself will one day reveal, Jesus is "the living Bread come down from heaven."[6] The flesh and blood of the Son of David will be food indeed and drink indeed for the life of a starving world.

Joseph has arranged this birth in Bethlehem, the City of David (since he is of the House of David), and it is through Joseph that Jesus is legally a *son* of David. Here on Christmas in

---

iii Keep in mind, the biblical account of the first Joseph takes place in Genesis, which means "beginning."

Bethlehem (which is Hebrew for "house of
bread"), the Bread of Life lies personified and
incarnate. His parents place him in a manger,
which is, precisely, a food trough. Joseph will
defend and protect this living Bread of Heaven
for the life of the world.

STUDY QUESTIONS:

1. *In what ways is St. Joseph like the patriarch
    Joseph in the Old Testament?*

2. *How is Joseph the patriarch of a "new Gen-
    esis"?*

3. *Re-read the last paragraph of this chapter. In
    what ways is Joseph the "Guardian of the Re-
    deemer"?*

Chapter Two

The Just Man: Who is He?

Of the early life of Joseph, his origins, his family, and his home life, we know very little with historical certainty. The biblical accounts give us a few facts (and these are limited mainly to the opening chapters of Matthew and Luke[i]). Yet sparse as they are, we are able to glean much precious data from them.

His name is an abbreviation of *Jehoseph*, which is Hebrew for, "May Yahweh give an increase." By lineage, Joseph descended from the House of David, and he was *probably* born in Bethlehem, the place where David was also born and raised, yet there is no absolute proof of this. It is, however, *probable* that some of his family and perhaps even some family property were there. We can deduce this from the fact that Joseph journeyed to Bethlehem for the census, and that upon his return from Egypt, he intended to take up residence there. The

---

[i] These are the so-called "Infancy Narratives."

census law required a person to enroll in the place where they held land.

Who was Joseph's father? The Gospels hold two genealogies of Christ. Luke's says Joseph's father was Heli.[1] Matthew's says it was Jacob.[2][ii] Keep in mind, we are not meant to read these family trees as we would our own. Rather, the authors have stylized and abbreviated them to lend their lists numerical significance, since this emphasized key theological and religious insights. We cannot go into the complex details, but the reader may wish to refer to the commentaries, among which Fr. Laurentin's[iii] will be most enlightening.[3]

For our purposes, we should make two points. First, Matthew's genealogy is descending, leading us from Abraham to Christ. Luke's is ascending, going from Christ through Abraham to God. As St. Augustine puts it,

---

[ii]   We read this latter lineage in Advent. The genealogy of Matthew, then, is a solemn liturgical moment for those who grasp that we are thereby proclaiming the human roots of the greatest birth ever celebrated in the history of the world. Doubtless, every time we approach another anniversary of the birth of Jesus, these blood lines echo in all their repetitive grandeur.

[iii] Fr. René Laurentin (b. 1917) is a French professor of Theology and one of the Church's greatest experts on Mary and Marian apparitions. One of the *periti* (experts) at the Second Vatican Council, he was the Council's primary author of its writings on Marian doctrine.

"One [evangelist] counts upward, the other downward, both count through Joseph."[4]

In an intricate manner, the second point answers the question, "Who was Joseph's father?" As we noted, Matthew says he was Jacob, but Luke says Heli. We know sacred Scripture cannot assert error, so we must make conjectures like all the Christian generations before us. Fr. Filas prefers to evoke the law of the "levirate" marriage.[5][iv] If a brother dies childless, another brother marries the widow to supply progeny. This was the most traditional solution. (Despite this, Fr. Laurentin disagrees and offers another theory you may want to read.[6]) If the levirate law was followed, Heli would have died childless but would be Joseph's legal father, while Jacob, a brother, would be Joseph's natural father. Jacob was of the line of

---

iv According to the 1913 *Catholic Encyclopedia*, a levirate marriage was "the marriage between a widow, whose husband had died childless, and her brother-in-law. She was, in fact, not permitted to marry a stranger, unless the surviving brother-in-law formally refused to marry her. The levirate marriage was intended first, to prevent the extinction of the name of the deceased childless brother; and secondly, to retain the property within the same tribe and family. The first-born son of such a union took the name of the deceased uncle instead of that of his father, and succeeded to his estate. If there were no brother of the deceased husband alive, then the next of kin was supposed to marry the widow as we find in the case of Ruth's relative who yielded his right to Boaz."

Solomon, and Heli of Nathan, but both lines
are of David.

   We also know the name of one of Joseph's
brothers, Cleophas.[v] St. John tells us "Mary
of Cleophas" stood with our Blessed Mother
beneath the cross. The designation "of
Cleophas" could mean she was his wife or his
daughter. Many Fathers of the Church hold
that Mary and Joseph were distant relatives.
Was Mary also a descendant of David? The
theologian Suárez[vi] insisted this was a matter
of Catholic Faith. Once more Fr. Laurentin
disagrees and gives his reasons,[7] and many other
reputable scholars agree with him.

   While we can never know the precise
nature of his genealogy, one thing is certain,
and this is our main concern: Joseph, as holy

---

[v] Scripture translations differ on the proper spelling of this
    man's name. In the Douai-Rheims, it is spelled as given
    here, while in the RSV and other translations, it is given
    as Clopas, Clophas, or Cleopas. The early Christian
    writers Papias and Hegesippus and the early Church
    historian Eusebius of Caesarea call him Joseph's brother.
    Additionally, he may also be one of the two disciples noted
    in Luke 24:18 who discussed the events of the Passion with
    Our Lord on the way to Emmaus.

[vi] Fr. Federico Suárez Verdeguer (March 30, 1917–January
    1, 2005) was a priest ordained in 1948 for the prelature
    of Opus Dei. He served as dean of the faculty of Arts at
    the University of Navarre from 1955–1960 and wrote a
    number of books, including *The Sacrifice of the Altar, Mary
    of Nazareth, Joseph of Nazareth,* and *When the Son of Man
    Comes.* A tireless worker, he died after preaching a retreat.

Scripture states, is "of the House of David."[8] This is why Scripture asserts Jesus' legal lineage from David through Joseph.

Joseph's trade

"Is not this the carpenter's son?"[9]

We receive this important fact of Joseph's profession later in Matthew's Gospel, and it possibly reveals for us what the biased hometown Nazarenes thought of Joseph. It almost has the air of a slur, a taunt against Jesus, Who had assumed the lowly trade of His father.[vii]

Though typically given as "carpenter," the inspired Greek word of this text is *tekton*. In itself, it literally means "craftsman," as does the early Latin translation, *faber*. Even into the ninth century, some writers interpreted it as "smith," which may have been a misunderstanding of allegories by some of the Fathers.

However, the great apologist St. Justin Martyr (born in Palestine circa 100 AD and therefore a most reliable source) informs us:

> When Jesus came to the Jordan, He was considered to be the son of Joseph the carpenter. He was deemed a carpenter when

---

vii Tending to back up Father's observation is that, according to Jim Bishop in his book *The Day Christ Died*, "an epithet of the Jews was to call a menial [i.e., a laborer] 'a cutter and a son of a cutter.'"

among men, making plows and yokes by
which He taught the symbols of righteousness
and an active life.[10]

Joseph worked with wood in making
cabinets, wheels, and farm and home furniture,
and he probably worked as a handyman. The
brilliant Origen[viii] speaks of the scorn of the
anti-Christian Celsus[ix] who referred to Christ's
woodwork. Julian the Apostate, a persecuting

[viii] Origen (ca. 185–ca. 254) was a Church Father and some
say the Church's first *bona fide* theologian. Probably from
Egypt, he taught in Alexandria, but was expelled by the
patriarch there because he received ordination without his
permission. After settling in Caesarea Maritima (a city now
in ruins between Tel Aviv and Haifa), he preached, taught,
and wrote, dying in a persecution of Christians. Despite
the fact that he is a Church Father and his writings are
considered incredibly important to this day, he held various
views that flatly contradicted orthodox Christianity. For
instance, he believed the three persons of the Trinity are
not equal but a hierarchy, with God the Father on top and
God the Holy Spirit at the bottom. He also taught universal
salvation, so that even the souls of the damned would
ultimately be saved, and he believed in the preexistence
of souls. Because of his teachings, the Second Council
of Constantinople (May 5-June 2, 553) declared him a
heretic.

[ix] Celsus was a late second century pagan and polemical
writer against Christianity. He intimated that Jesus made
up the virgin birth to hide the fact that he was conceived
in "unsavory circumstances." He called the Christians
religiously and politically intolerant, and he thought
the doctrines of the Incarnation and Crucifixion were
abhorrent.

emperor, spoke in contempt of Jesus, "He is making a coffin for your burial."

Another allegorical theme frequently used by the Fathers plays on "carpenter" and "wood of the cross." Because of this and other allusions, St. Augustine held Joseph up as a model for laboring monks.

STUDY QUESTIONS:

1. *Considering all of this, how is Joseph a model for you?*

2. *What is it that made Joseph a "just man"?*

3. *Read paragraph 437 of the Catechism of the Catholic Church. What is Joseph's role and calling?*

4. *Read Matthew 1:20–21. What is Joseph's "Annunciation"?*

5. *How can this chapter's reflections aid you in your own role as a worker?*

CHAPTER THREE

THE TESTING

If it is true that we have few details of Joseph's external life, we know even less of his interior, moral life. We can, however, make logical deductions from the scriptural facts, and they are rich indeed. All are summed up in that phrase in Matthew 1:19, that Joseph was "a just man."

We must keep this adjective in mind as we continue our reflections. In the Bible, being "just" expresses the height of sanctity, a most perfect relationship of the soul with God and man.

The betrothed

We know nothing explicit about how Joseph and Mary came to be betrothed. Her family was in Nazareth,[1] while Joseph's family possibly had its origin in Bethlehem. Perhaps there was, as some suggest, some remote degree of kinship with Mary's family. Maybe Joseph had come to the area for work as nearby communities were growing and construction work was plentiful. However the betrothal came to be, we would be far off track if we thought of it in terms of modern "courtship."

In any event, at some point and in some unknown way, Joseph and Mary met, their families made an agreement, and there followed a chaste friendship. Many have heard of the legend of the flowering staff of Joseph. Supposedly, he contended with other suitors for Mary's hand and was chosen only by divine intervention through the aforementioned budding rod. (This is where we get the image in religious art.)

In this detail, we see an attempt to link it with the blooming stump of Jesse and the Messianic Spirit in Isaiah,[2] and/or the flowering rod of Aaron.[3] (Anne Catherine Emmerich also speaks of it.) Some, however, say this could not have happened because it would have broken the otherwise intact pattern of "normalcy" that we see in Joseph's life (which we will explain shortly). Such an event would have caused public admiration from the start.

Returning to the question of betrothal, two stages of marriage were customary at the time these two saints lived.

The first was the espousal, when a man and woman were officially betrothed. This engagement, which the law already considered a true marriage, lasted about a full year, and the couple lived separately during this period.

In the past, most Catholic scholars believed this espousal period conferred full matrimonial rights. This notion, however, was based on a misunderstanding of certain texts of the *Mishnah*.[i] More recent studies have shown that marital relations of the espoused were considered disgraceful and immoral and were at the very least frowned upon.

Considering this, it is probable that the Annunciation occurred no earlier than the eighth month of espousal, since there were no external signs of Mary's pregnancy at the time of the second stage, the solemnization of the marriage, when the couple began to live in common.

If the Holy Couple observed contemporary Jewish custom, Mary was about twelve-and-a-half-years old at the time of her espousal to Joseph. As for Joseph, the norm for the man was 18 or 19 years of age. All this, of course, runs contrary to the traditional thought (again influenced by the apocrypha). Many of our holy pictures and statues portray Joseph as strikingly older than Mary with gray or white hair and

---

[i] The *Mishnah* is the collection of the early Jewish oral traditions and commentaries on Scripture. They were compiled circa 200 AD.

beard. The motive for this theologized art was to proclaim clearly the virginity of Mary before and after the miraculous conception and birth of Jesus. Such, too, were the motives behind the incorrect exaggerations in the apocrypha, which all portrayed Joseph as advanced in years. Some even scandalously depicted him as a decrepit, senile widower with a number of children.

However, believers and scoffers alike well know the fact that the orthodox Catholic Faith teaches the Virgin Birth of Jesus and Mary's perpetual virginity. It therefore in no way contradicts this Faith (and is even proper and probable) to assert the youth of Joseph at the time of his marriage. After all, his mission required youthful vigor, not the loss of faculties associated with old age.

Furthermore, if we look at Scripture, the whole pattern of divine action in the Holy Family is that of a normal Palestinian family, thereby cloaking the Incarnation until Jesus Christ later decides to reveal it. If Mary and Joseph were not of a normal age for marriage, this exception would have aroused speculation, if not scornful wonderment.

The Gethsemane of Joseph

When Mary ... had been betrothed to Joseph, before they came together, she was found to be with child by the Holy Spirit. But Joseph her husband, being a just man, and not wishing to expose her to reproach, was minded to put her away privately.[4]

One of Joseph's most crucial experiences is his "dark night" (often called his Gethsemane) when he was made aware of Mary's pregnancy. The Annunciation, when "the Word was made flesh," must have taken place in the last quarter of the year of betrothal. Catholic scholars have traditionally believed Mary had taken a vow of virginity. Recall her words, "I do not know man." This statement *suggests* but admittedly does not *prove* such a vow.

However, Mary would not have asked the question if she had expected to enjoy normal marital relations with Joseph in the near future. Otherwise, she could have thought, "When I conceive by Joseph, God will make our child the Messiah." Doubtless, the young couple must have discussed and mutually agreed upon this most essential element of their future life.

Shortly after the Annunciation, Mary left Nazareth to visit and assist her cousin Elizabeth. The traditional home of Zechariah and Elizabeth is Ein Kerem, a small village nestled in the hills about four-to-five miles west of Jerusalem. Mary's journey, therefore, entailed about 83 miles of arduous travel. Who chaperoned this adolescent girl? Surely, someone accompanied her. Was it Joseph?

After three months, John the Baptist was born, and Mary returned home from her mission of charity. Now the dilemma painfully arose in her heart. Soon her pregnancy would become visible and precisely at the time the marriage was to be solemnized. Mary had to make her condition known to Joseph before they lived together. It would have been unjust and unloving to do otherwise.

Yet she felt bound not to reveal on her own the mystery of the Incarnation, for only God could credibly announce such an awesome event. Mary knew the terrible agony her message would cause Joseph. Perhaps soon after her return from Ein Kerem, Mary decided she would communicate the *fact* but not the *cause* of her divine secret. She could not allow the visible evidence to anticipate her words. Did Mary do this herself or through a confidante, perhaps her dear mother Anne? Fr. Filas sees St. Anne fulfilling this delicate mission.[5]

What is certain is that a sword pierced the pure heart of Joseph. We variously name this crisis the "testing," the "doubt," or the "hesitation" of Joseph. In any case, he must have experienced a very human bewilderment.

A quick point: The term "doubt" could

easily be misunderstood. Joseph never doubted Mary's purity and fidelity. On the other hand, nor could he, as a true man, whisk away the fact that in every case he knew, pregnancy occurred as a consequence of carnal knowledge. Was this, then, some astounding, unique, spiritual exception, one unheard of through all human history?

We should also note one of the rabbinic laws on espousal as they refer to the wife. If she is unfaithful, she incurs the laws of adultery. Now the laws of adultery required public denunciation, a bill of divorce, and, at least in theory, the Mosaic prescription of a death penalty.[6]

What was Joseph, the "just man," to do? How long did he endure this excruciating mental torment? He never doubted Mary's purity, nor did he doubt God's omnipotence and providence. Nevertheless, Joseph was a man, yes, a young man. He had no precedent in human history to guide him. Yet such was his conviction of her purity that he could not suspect Mary had been unfaithful. Look at what the unknown author of a commentary incorrectly attributed to St. John Chrysostom wrote:

> O inestimable tribute to Mary! Joseph believed in her chastity more than in her womb, in grace more than in nature! He

plainly saw the conception, and he was
incapable of suspecting fornication. He
believed that it was more possible for a
woman to conceive without a man than for
Mary to be able to sin.[7]

Suárez showed that the Church Fathers took
two general approaches. Some said Joseph was
convinced of adultery and that he was wronged.
However, he determined to bear this patiently
without any recrimination or public recourse
to penalties. They saw this as an act of great
virtue.

To quote Suárez, the second interpretation
was:

Joseph was unable to judge or suspect the
Virgin harshly. Influenced in one direction
by the factual evidence he perceived, but
swayed in the other by the exalted sanctity
of the Virgin as he knew it from experience,
he withheld all judgment because he was
overwhelmed by a kind of stupefaction and
great wonder. It was indeed a consummate
act of justice to be carried out of himself in
so grave a matter, nor [was he] blinded by
extreme passion or feeling. He persuaded
himself that the event could have occurred
without sin. Consequently he was unwilling
to expose Mary; but since for him nothing in

the matter was sufficiently clear, he believed
that it pertained to justice to be separated
from such a woman and to dismiss her in
secret.[8]

This second line of understanding
certainly has to be preferred. In no way could
we rationalize the justice of Joseph if he knew
Mary was adulterous and did not follow the
prescriptions of the law. After all, he never
acted outside the existing law in other matters.
Nor, on the other hand, should Joseph, the chief
witness of Mary's purity, have ever harbored a
conviction of so grave a sin.

The three months of the Visitation were a
magnificent touch of God's Providence. During
this awkward time, even if Joseph had escorted
her, Mary was likely spared almost all close
encounters with her spouse. Note also that it
was expressly at this time of the "testing" and
on this very matter that in the text cited above,
St. Matthew calls Joseph, "just."

As Fr. Filas notes, people throughout the
centuries have hailed Joseph's action in this
regard as "his absolutely firm witness to the
virginity of our Lady."[9] For instance, St. Jerome[ii]

[ii] St. Jerome (c. 347–September 30, 420) was a Church Father
who is best known for translating the Bible into Latin from
original sources. This version, called the Vulgate (so-called
because Latin was the "vulgar," i.e., common language), is

says, "This is evidence that Joseph, knowing
Mary's chastity and wondering at what had
occurred, concealed in silence the mystery he
did not fathom."[10]

How long did Joseph's testing last? Fr.
Filas says, "In all likelihood no more than two
weeks," adding that a more protracted agony
might have threatened the bond of love by the
trauma of psychological pain involved.[11]

In this, Joseph's "Gethsemane," there are
spiritual lessons for us.

Catholics today often suffer similar though
far less acute trials. For example, the media often
barrages us with inaccurate and contradictory
reports that tend to undermine our faith in the
Magisterium or in our Holy Father's words
and decisions. When this happens, even when
the evidence presented us seems damningly
convincing, we must never harbor doubts
against the Church's teachings. Like St. Joseph,
we must hold fast to our Faith, knowing there
must be and will be a clarification.

Throughout the biblical record, we see
parallels to Joseph's severe trial that show this is
the way God chooses to purify those He loves.
Among these we might mention:

---

still the normative Bible used by the Church for approved
Catholic translations.

- The testing of Abraham when ordered by God to sacrifice his son Isaac.
- The testing of Joseph of Egypt, extending the type of the two Josephs. Psalm 105 says of the first Joseph, "Until what he said came to pass, the word of the Lord tested him."
- The agony of Jesus in the Garden of Gethsemane.
- The excruciating sorrow of Mary at Christ's death.

STUDY QUESTIONS:

1. *What were the two stages of marriage for Jews at the time of Joseph and Mary? At which stage were couples considered truly married?*

2. *What are the arguments for and against Joseph's youth or advanced age?*

3. *Why do you think some call the episode in Matthew 1:18–19 "Joseph's Gethsemane"? What would you have done in his place?*

4. *What does Joseph's response to Mary's news teach us in light of the negative portrayal the media often gives the Church?*

5. *At the end of the chapter, Fr. Gilsdorf notes several points about how God chooses to purify those He loves. What parallels do you see between these biblical episodes and "Joseph's Gethsemane"?*

CHAPTER FOUR

JOSEPH THE MOST CHASTE SPOUSE

Joseph's torment was finally brought to a merciful and happy end by the message of an angel delivered to him in a special dream:

> While he thought on these things, behold, an angel of the Lord appeared to him in a dream saying, "Be not afraid, Joseph, son of David, to take to thee Mary thy wife, for that which is begotten in her is of the Holy Spirit."[1]

Just as an angel held Abraham's hand at the last moment of his testing, when ordered to sacrifice Isaac, his only-begotten beloved son,[2] so now an angel spared and illuminated Joseph before he carried out the conscientious decision to divorce her quietly.

Now the solemnization of the marriage could take place at the customary time. The text indicates that Joseph, as always, moved to it immediately. "So Joseph, arising from sleep, did what the angel of the Lord had commanded him and took unto him his wife."[3]

They would have held a public celebration. According to custom, Joseph would have gone with his friends to Mary's home to claim her as his bride and to bring her in procession to his house.

Notice the words of this new state, "live together ... take to yourself."[4] We can figure this comes from the customs of the time, but Scripture is silent and thus leaves us wondering about details. We do not know whether Joseph had his home in Nazareth or somewhere else more remote. Fr. Gaechter situated the journey to Bethlehem and residence there at this juncture. We prefer to imagine a northern residence despite the problem of the notoriety of Mary's being with child. Of course, a significant result of the marriage is that Joseph thereby accepted Jesus as his Son.

In the fourth century, St. Augustine made the first full study of this union and concluded it was a true marriage:

> "The virginal motherhood simultaneous with conception within marriage could only mean the existence of a *virginal marriage*."[5]

St. Ignatius of Antioch says that, by reason of such a unique but genuine marriage, "the virginity of Mary was hidden from the Prince of the world [i.e., the devil]."[6] The Fathers frequently voiced this important theme, and St. Thomas Aquinas lists it as one of his 12 reasons why Christ chose to be born of an espoused virgin.

> "By means of the espousal, Joseph's testimony proved that Christ was born of a virgin."[7]

We should also meditate on this passage from St. Bernard of Clairvaux:

> I will say what seems to me to be correct as it did to the Fathers before me. The reason for Mary's espousal was the reason for Thomas' doubt. Just as Thomas by doubting and handling Christ became the most irrefutable witness of the Lord's resurrection, so was Joseph an irrefutable witness of Mary's chastity by becoming her spouse and by carefully approving her mode of life during the time she was in his custody. And just as I who am weak would offer my belief in the resurrection of the Son because of Thomas who doubted and handled the Savior, rather than because of Cephas who heard and believed, so would I more easily believe the virginity of the mother because of the spouse who guarded her and put her to the test than because of the virgin who defends

herself according to her own conscience. Necessarily, therefore, was Mary espoused to Joseph since by this means the holy thing was hidden from the dogs, her virginity was attested by her spouse, and the exalted modesty of the virgin was spared as well as her honor safeguarded. What is more wise, what more excellent, than Divine Providence! By this one design a witness is initiated into celestial secrets, the enemy is excluded from them, and the honor of the virgin is preserved intact. Otherwise, when would a just man have spared an adulteress? Since he was just, he was unwilling to manifest her. Since he would not have been just if he had consented to one who was known to be guilty, so by no means would he have been just if he had condemned proved innocence.[8]

Returning now to the 12 reasons of St. Thomas, we will cite two more. Christ chose to be born of an espoused virgin because it showed forth "the mystical union of Christ and the Church." Moreover, it "also shows God blesses equally marriage and virginity as states of life to refute later heretics impugning one or the other."[9]

Thus, by the solemnization of the marriage, Joseph now enters into the mystery of the Incarnation. For this, there must be a parallel between the mission of Mary and that of Joseph. Mary was prepared for her role by superlative gifts of sanctity; she was filled with grace. We can therefore safely assert that Joseph was likewise prepared by an infusion of grace and sanctity second only to those of his spouse. Mary is virgin and mother; Joseph is virgin and (in the sense we will later clarify) father. This unique but genuine marriage, therefore, upholds the sanctity both of marriage and of virginity.

In *Quamquam Pluries*, Pope Leo XIII states, "Marriage is the closest possible union and relationship whereby each spouse mutually participates in the good of the other."[i] As the Pope insists, the *spiritual union* is the most critically important element in marriage. Without it, the *physical union* is devoid of its meaning and debased. In a sense, this is the essence of John Paul II's Theology of the Body.

A virginal marriage

At this point it will be helpful to stress the virginity of this marriage—both that of Mary and of Joseph. Protestants often cite several seemingly problematic scriptural passages in an

---

[i] *Quamquam Pluries*, no. 3. This text is also translated as, "For marriage is the most intimate of all unions which from its essence imparts a community of gifts between those that by it are joined together."

effort to disprove that virginity. This problem is readily solved once the texts are studied in the original Greek and Aramaic words from Jewish sources. The Greek, moreover, is the inspired text whose precise meaning is not fully evident when translated into modern vernacular languages.

So let us look at the first "problem" text.

> "And he did not know her till she brought forth her firstborn son."[10]

Unlike our English adverb "till," the Semitic usage that underlies the text does not at all suggest any change after a certain period. It merely states a fact of what was the case *until* that time. Greek usage is similar. The "till" in no way indicates that sexual relations took place after Our Lord's birth.

Let us look at two other biblical examples. The first is, "For He must reign until He has put all His enemies under His feet."[11] Does He cease reigning after this happens?

The second is, "Michal [daughter of Saul] had no child until the day of her death."[12] But what? She had a bevy of babies afterward?

The next potential problem in the text comes from the term "first born." This is a technical, legal title for the first male child born of a marriage. Abundant biblical evidence proves that it in no way asserts whether there were or were not other children.

For instance, writing in the fourth century, St. Jerome deals perfectly with this term:

> From this passage certain people have perversely conjectured that Mary had other sons, for they assert that he alone is to be called "first-born" who has brothers. However, it is customary in Holy Scripture to call "first-born" not him whom brothers follow, but him who is first begotten.[13]

Let us follow St. Jerome a bit further since he will shed much light on our subject:

> But just as we do not deny what is written, we do reject what is not written. That God was born of a virgin, we believe because we read it. That Mary consummated marriage after her childbirth we do not believe because we do not read it. Nor do we say this in order to condemn marriage—for virginity itself is a fruit of marriage—but because there is no license to draw false conclusions about holy men. Nor (if we wish to take the mere possibility into consideration) can we contend that Joseph had several wives because Abraham and Jacob had several wives, and that from these wives the brethren of the Lord were born, a fiction which most people

invent with not so much pious motives as
presumptuous audacity. You say Mary did
not remain a virgin: Even more do I claim
that Joseph also was virginal through Mary,
in order that from a virginal marriage a
virginal son might be born. For if the charge
of fornication does not fall on this holy man,
and if it is not written that he had another
wife, and if he was more a protector than a
husband of Mary, whom he was thought to
have (as his wife), it remains to assert that he
who merited to be called the father of the
Lord remained virginal with her.[14]

With its highly convincing force, this
argument also helps us deal with a third problem
phrase, the several Gospel references to the
brethren of Jesus (e.g., Mark 3:31–35, Mark
6:1–6, Matt 13:55–57).

Here once more we must understand the
Semitic usage of this phrase in no way proves
they were blood brothers and sisters of Jesus
from the union of Mary and Joseph. This phrase
commonly embraced all near relatives, such as
cousins, nephews, and so on.[ii] While we cannot
pursue this argument, the Gospels contain

[ii] See Gen 14:14, where Lot is called Abraham's "brother"
in the Douai-Rheims, Young's Literal Translation, King
James Version, Darby Translation, and many others, even
though he was clearly a nephew.

numerous indications that Jesus was indeed the sole Child of the Holy Family.

John's Gospel, for instance, tells us that on the cross, Jesus entrusts His mother to the young apostle John as her son. If the "brothers of Jesus" mentioned in the Gospel were blood sons of Mary, John's blessed custody would not have been required. Indeed, it would have been scandalous.

It is true that some Catholics in the early centuries relied on the "wife and children of Joseph" theme found in the apocrypha. This was especially true of the Eastern Church where the apocrypha had an exceptional influence. Even Fathers like Hilary, Gregory of Nyssa, and Ambrose used this facile explanation.[iii]

We return, therefore, to St. Jerome, who expresses strong opposition to this opinion:

> Certain people who follow the ravings[iv] of the apocrypha fancy that the brethren of the Lord are sons of Joseph from another wife and invent a certain woman, Melch or Escha. As it is contained in the book which we wrote against Helvidius, we understand as brethren

---

[iii] St. Hilary lived ca. 300–368, St. Gregory of Nyssa lived from ca. 335 until after 394, and St. Ambrose of Milano lived from c. 338–April 4, 397.

[iv] The Latin here is *deliramenta*. It also means nonsense, delusion, absurdity, or madness.

of the Lord not the sons of Joseph but the
cousins of the Savior, children of Mary—the
Lord's maternal aunt—who is said to be the
mother of James the Less and Joseph and Jude
who, as we read, were called brethren of the
Lord in another passage of the Gospel. Indeed
all Scripture indicates that cousins are called
brethren.

Other Fathers and theologians firmly
asserted the same, among whom was the
previously mentioned Origen, an expert in
oriental languages.

St. Augustine, who reports both conjectures,
shows his preference in beautiful sentences in
his sermons:

> "His greater purity made his fatherhood
> secure."

> "He was so much more truly the father as he
> was virginally the father."

> "Just as he was virginally the husband, so he
> was virginally the father."[15]

In ensuing centuries, the solid teaching
of Jerome dominated most theologians as they
discussed these delicate areas. The eleventh
century Doctor St. Peter Damian voiced what

turned out to be a watershed in the affirmation of Joseph's perpetual virginity:

> Do you not know that the Son of God preferred the purity of the flesh to such an extent that He became man in the closed womb of a virgin rather than in the respectability of marriage? And if it does not suffice for you that not only the mother is a virgin, there remains the belief of the Church that he who served as father is also a virgin.[16]

This view became the consensus among Catholic scholars. The legends did linger on in some devotional books that affected popular notions for some time after. However, as Thomas Aquinas's teacher St. Albert the Great said:

> Joseph is called Mary's husband. By his solicitude he was like a father; by his espousal he was like a husband; by his protection of chastity he was the guide of virginity…. What sort of ordinance of Divine Wisdom would choose an unclean witness and protector for the virgin mother?[17]

STUDY QUESTIONS:

1. *What are several of the emotions Joseph likely felt upon hearing the angel's message? How would you have felt?*

2. *Read Matthew 1:24, Matthew 2:13–14, and Matthew 2:20–21. What insight into Joseph's personality do these passages indicate?*

3. *Why does St. Ignatius of Antioch believe "the virginity of Mary was hidden from the prince of this world" (i.e., Satan)? How might this relate to Genesis 3:15?*

4. *Why does the phrase in Matthew 1:25 not indicate Mary had other children or normal marital relations?*

5. *What are the arguments Fr. Gilsdorf gives for Joseph's own virginity?*

CHAPTER FIVE

THE GREATEST JOURNEY

And Joseph went from Galilee out of the town of Nazareth into Judea to the town of David, which is called Bethlehem—because he was of the house and family of David—to register, together with Mary his espoused wife, who was with child.[1]

The Bible is laced with special journeys. Think how our father in faith Abraham journeyed from Ur along the arc of the Fertile Crescent to what we now call Israel.[i] Even more pivotal was the Exodus, where Moses led the Hebrews out of Egypt, a journey that is a type of our Christian redemption and is consistently echoed in the Gospels.

Then there was the Jews' joyous return from

---

[i] According *to The Columbia Encyclopedia* (Sixth Edition, Columbia University Press), the Fertile Crescent is a "well-watered and fertile area [that] arcs across the northern part of the Syrian desert. It is flanked on the west by the Mediterranean and on the east by the Euphrates and Tigris rivers, and includes all or parts of Israel, the West Bank, Jordan, Lebanon, Syria, and Iraq."

their Babylonian captivity, made possible by
the tolerance decree of the conquering Persian
Emperor Cyrus (559 BC–529 BC). There are
others on a smaller scale that are also significant
in a religious and symbolic sense.

We have already mentioned the virtuous
mission of the pregnant Mary when she rose up
in haste to visit and assist her cousin Elizabeth
in Ein Kerem.

But of all these travels, only one deserves
to be called the greatest, the holiest, and the
loveliest of all: The journey to Bethlehem.
Perhaps we should call it a procession.

Earlier we mentioned the chronology
proposed by Fr. Gaechter. He conjectures—from
reasons of suitability—that Joseph prudently
made this journey to Bethlehem very soon after
his formal marriage to Mary. The motive, he
believes, was to spare Mary from the questions
of the inquisitive Nazarenes once her pregnancy
became visible. We later learn that the people of
this village were capable of angry rejection of
Jesus—"Is not this the carpenter's son?"[2]

Another argument to favor the theory of
an early arrival (rather than their arriving just
before Jesus' birth) is that in the final weeks of
gestation, Mary would have traveled the long
rugged way with great discomfort and danger.

While this early date sounds logical and

prudent, it would place the journey several months before the birth of Jesus. In this scenario, Joseph took Mary directly to Bethlehem, where he was able to obtain temporary housing and make advance preparations by his labor.

Once Mary reached her term and the birth was imminent, Joseph sought more suitable shelter and privacy. He failed to find shelter in private homes. The inn itself was no place for them in the sense that privacy and decorum were impossible, so he found refuge for them in the stable of the inn.

This is possible. It does not contradict the Gospel account nor does it fail to recognize the zeal, love, and prudence of Joseph. Nonetheless, it all remains mere conjecture.

Other less drastic solutions to the obvious problems could be offered. Perhaps Joseph owned or established temporary quarters elsewhere in the north. The acclaimed Fr. René Laurentin calls Fr. Gaechter's work "the most daring and painstaking reconstruction," yet his conclusion is as follows:

> As interesting and penetrating as the many observations of Gaechter may be, the reconstruction belongs in the realm of science-fiction. The author boldly reconstructs the events: Mary, betrothed in October 9 BC, went to Bethlehem immediately after her

marriage with Joseph, five months before
the birth of Jesus, which Gaechter located in
March 7 BC.

Some readers may not be aware that the first
Christmas did occur some years before 1 AD.
We only mark Christ's birth in that year because
of miscalculations by the monk Dionysius
Exiguus (c. 470–c. 544), who was entrusted
with revision of the calendar.

Complex as these considerations may be,
pondering all this seems very helpful even in our
booklet of meditations since it often highlights
the overlooked problems and decisions Joseph
had to face.

Nevertheless, we will be on safer footing
to follow the simpler, traditional interpretation
suggested by the inspired biblical data that has
nourished pious reflection throughout the
centuries.

The route of the journey was probably the
same as that taken in the Visitation, which Luke
tells us was through the hill country known as
the *shephelah*, a geographical backbone down the
center of Israel.[ii] The other routes were safer and
more level, but this was the more direct route,
and significantly, it was trodden by the feet of
countless pious pilgrims going up to Jerusalem

[ii]   This is also the route that King David took with the Ark of
the Covenant in 2 Sam 6:2-16.

for the great Temple feasts. The distance to Jerusalem was about 85 miles. Joseph, however, was going five miles further south to Bethlehem to register in his ancestral home as required by the imperial census.

We can be sure that Joseph set a prudent daily pace out of respect for Mary's condition that added one more penitential aspect to this pilgrimage. Perhaps, then, about two weeks were required. These very weeks would correspond to our final phase of Advent. The earlier weeks were the period of prayerful preparation.

We can meditate on these preparations with great spiritual gain. As an expectant mother, Mary prepared the customary necessities for her Child. We hear only of the swaddling clothes, but she doubtless had many other items to gather or to make with her own hands.

The spiritual preparations, however, would have been the most sublime experiences. Every expectant mother lives in constant awareness of the new life stirring in her womb. She must make sacrifices big and small and perform other acts of self-denial, all for the advantage of her child. She does so with joy, and—if she is a believer—she will give thanks and pray for the life within.

But Mary heightens these universal maternal experiences in correspondence with her exalted

holiness and her knowledge of the mystery of
Who this Child of hers is. For her, the first
Advent was filled with love, self-giving, peace,
joy, and a constant inward contemplation. Hers
was not only hope, but literally expectation,
longing to behold the face of this Child, hers
and God's. We recall the salutation of Gabriel,
"Hail, full of grace, the Lord is with thee"… is
within thee!

In his own way, Joseph shared in this loving
preparation. He, too, must have meditated on and
adored the Child in Mary's womb. Enlightened
now by heavenly revelation, he knew that his
young wife was "blessed among women" and
that "the fruit of her womb" was blessed, the
Holy One of God. As a man with a mission
to be the Redeemer's protector and provider,
he labored arduously to assemble provisions for
the journey. He would have carefully planned
ahead to meet every need, and to attempt to
estimate the daily schedule, to plot the possible
night-shelters.

Then the day came for departure on the
journey south to Bethlehem. Each day of this
procession, Mary, like a living monstrance, rode
astride the donkey, with Joseph walking along
side holding the reins. Each night, he would
have needed to have found shelter. Perhaps they
stayed in roadside inns? The homes of friends and

relatives? But surely, most often, the carpenter had to improvise, cutting and assembling branches to construct a lean-to. Nights in any desert are usually chilled, anyway, but given the time frame, this was also the traditional season of the cold winter rains.

On all sides were threats and terrors. Wild animals still ranged the wooded hilly areas.[iii] Other predators, equally cunning and merciless, were the notorious robber bands who scouted the trail for pilgrims to plunder. The courage, skills, and resourcefulness of Joseph are given wordless witness by the fact that this newly married couple not only made the journey but made it safely (undoubtedly with the protection of many angels).

In the daytime, there was the tedium of ascending hills and traversing valleys. As any woman who has endured the extreme discomfort of a late term will attest, this would have caused Mary extreme discomfort. This suffering must have struck a pained, compassionate response in her loving spouse. Bystanders probably observed them quickly and shrugged. Just a young man and his young, pregnant wife and nothing more. Who would have dreamed that before their eyes

---

iii Keep in mind that before the Romans denuded the Middle East and northern Africa of them for gladiatorial games, these areas were home to lions and bears.

had just passed their Messiah, the Anointed
longed for from the ages? Even less could they
discern that the Messiah was truly "Emmanuel,
God with us," the very Son of God. Scripture
foretold that a virgin would conceive and bear a
Son, and this was that very virgin!

Try as we might, the prayers and
conversation of Mary and Joseph inevitably
escape our powers of imagination. What did
they share? How much did Joseph advance in
holiness during this Advent?

We may conjecture further about the last
miles as they approached their destination.
Would Mary and Joseph have chosen to bypass
Ein Kerem, which was directly on their path?
It was situated two miles north of Jerusalem.
Can we suppose that, had they stopped there,
the place where Mary had so recently aided her
cousin in her own recent pregnancy, that there
would have been a grand reception? Can we
permit ourselves to picture the possibility of
a reunion of the priest Zechariah and his wife
Elizabeth with Mary and Joseph, with little John
sleeping in their midst? If this happened—and
again Scripture doesn't mention it—Mary and
Joseph would have had a day or so of rest and
nourishment, some much needed warmth and
comfort in the generous company of Zechariah

and Elizabeth. They also would have had the chance to replenish their supplies.

Despite the silence of the Gospel account, we will dare add one more rather plausible conjecture. Jerusalem lay directly on the path to Bethlehem. Would Mary and Joseph have failed to enter the Holy City? If so, would they not have paid a visit to the Temple? What a fulfillment that would have been! The Holy of Holies had been vacant for centuries. The Ark of the Covenant vanished when the Temple was destroyed at the time of the deportation in 587 BC.

But dare we imagine that Mary, the new Ark of the Covenant, enters the new Temple? Within her womb resides the *Shekinah* of the Tabernacle.[iv] God's only begotten Son fills the Temple with a real incarnate divine Presence. He was in His Father's house.

One might construct another scenario. Perhaps a departure from Ein Kerem in the early morning, a visit to the Temple later in the morning after a two mile walk, about noon, and a final deadline to be met—five miles of rather desolate travel slightly southwest to Bethlehem!

And thou, Bethlehem, of the land of Judah,

[iv] The *Shekinah*—or *Sh'cheenah*—was the dwelling or the very Presence of God.

art by no means least among the princes of
Judah; for from thee shall come forth a leader
who shall rule My people Israel.³

Then, as the afternoon shadows lengthened
into evening, Joseph began his search for a
proper place for Mary, whose hour had come.
Some scholars have suggested reading "the
inn was no place for them," rather than "there
was no place for them in the inn."⁴ᵛ The need
was admittedly not just for any shelter, but
for privacy and propriety. Yet the traditional
meditation is forever valid: The heartsick

ᵛ Some scholars go beyond this. They say that the word
commonly translated as "inn"—*katalyma*—is actually
best understood as a room set apart, a private room. The
same word is used in Luke 22:11 ("And you shall say to the
goodman of the house, 'The master says to you: Where is
the *guest chamber* [or *guest room*] where I may eat the pasch
with My disciples?'"). The theory here is that such a room
was needed for childbirth, since, due to the blood loss
associated with delivering a baby, a woman was ritually
unclean for 40–80 days after a birth (depending on whether
she bore a boy or a girl). Furthermore, anyone who came
in contact with a childbearing mother was also ritually
unclean. Since Bethlehem was Joseph's town, and since
he likely would have had relatives there, and since those
relatives would have likely been inundated with other
relatives like Joseph, the house would have been quite full.
According to this theory, anyone in it would have risked
ritual contamination by Mary's delivery. As a result, Mary
and Joseph actively sought a less intrusive place (such as the
stable attached to the house) and had the baby Jesus there.
Again, this is only a theory, but it is an interesting one.

Joseph on the first Christmas Eve knocking on doors and hearts was repeatedly rejected; Mary waiting prayerfully, quietly abandoned to God's providence, astride that blessed noble donkey; the Child within her about to be born. "He came to His own, and His own received Him not."[5] People closed their doors in the face of the Creator, Savior, and Judge of the universe. It was a prophetic forecast of so many rejections in all the generations yet to come.

The Advent application good Christians have always drawn was to listen for Joseph's knocking and his plea to open the doors of our homes and hearts for Mary and her Child. "To those who did receive Him, He gave them power to become children of God."[6]

We move now in spirit to the refuge, probably a combination cave/stable used by shepherds like those still seen in the area, a place to shelter themselves and their flocks. We see Joseph busily and artfully preparing the place of delivery and the manger/crib for the Infant.

At this point we return to our opening reflections—Joseph the patriarch of the new and everlasting covenant, guardian and custodian of the Bread from heaven. God has appointed him "Lord of His house and prince of all His possessions."[7] The earthly father provides.

In the depth of the night, Mary gives birth.

The purest eyes on earth, undimmed by sin, look with maternal ecstasy into the eternal depths of the little eyes of her Divine Son, Who is also the Son of God, eyes now looking outward with infinite love into the world He created in the beginning.

Then Joseph approaches. His chaste, fatherly eyes gaze in rapture on the face of the Christ Child. As a sure guide of the journey to Bethlehem, that "House of Bread," he has accomplished his first task. Soon there would be more journeys of pilgrimage and exile: the Presentation of the Infant, the coming of the Magi, the flight into Egypt, and years later, the finding of his Boy in the Temple. How can we not give to this Christmas procession the title of "The Greatest Journey"? And Joseph led the way.

What a powerful lesson to the youth of all times! If we hold the more common modern view of the age of the Holy Couple, does it not become irresistibly appealing to the good young people living among us? Will they not perhaps be astonished and thrilled to discover how God entrusted the salvation of the world into the care of a very young man and woman? Will they not open their hearts to the call and challenge of God to undertake great missions that He has in store for *them* in the Church?

STUDY QUESTIONS:

1. *Why do you think Fr. Gilsdorf calls Mary and Joseph's journey to Bethlehem a "procession"?*

2. *What are the arguments for and against the Holy Couple's early arrival in Bethlehem?*

3. *What do you think were some of the ways Joseph and Mary prepared for the birth of their Son, both individually and as a couple?*

4. *Using the example of the Holy Couple, how do we open our hearts to God's call to undertake the great missions He has in store for us in the Church?*

CHAPTER SIX

FROM BETHLEHEM TO NAZARETH

*And when eight days were fulfilled
for His Circumcision, His name was called
Jesus, the name given Him by the angel
before He was conceived in the womb.*[1]

Throughout their earthly life, the Holy
Family carefully observed all the
prescriptions of the Law of Moses. St. Luke
repeatedly calls attention to their obedience in
the events that we will consider below.[2] Thus
on the octave day of His birth, the parents have
their infant Son sealed in the flesh with the sign
of the Old Covenant. The precious blood is
shed for the first time and the name "Jesus" is
conferred, just as the angel had prescribed: Jesus,
Yeshua,[i] the Savior, a name that foreshadows the
universal salvation in His blood drained for us

---

[i]   Yeshua is Jesus' name in Aramaic and Hebrew. In English,
     we would say, "Joshua." The name means, "God saves."

on the cross, even the very last drops from His heart.

What was Joseph's role in this sacred rite? Fr. Filas suggests that out of reverence for the Divine Infant, Joseph himself performed the circumcision usually done by a religious official of the village.[3] This, however, is speculation. What is far more certain is that Joseph bestowed the sacred name of Jesus upon the Child. This was the father's role,[4] and Joseph was the legal father.

We cannot emphasize enough that the Holy Family *seemed* an ordinary Jewish family. The Fathers teach that this had to be the case since the divine purpose was to conceal the mystery of the Incarnation until Christ revealed it in His public ministry. We have already referred to this pattern, which we might call, "the principle of normalcy."

Joseph the father

We must now consider in what sense Joseph can be called Jesus' father.

St. Luke informs us in his genealogy that "Jesus Himself, when He began His work, was about 30 years of age, being—as was thought (*ut putabatur*) the son of Joseph...."[5] Hence we sometimes hear him called "the putative father of Jesus" or Jesus' "foster father."

However, Luke's language in no way militates against a true fatherhood. Rather, he merely reinforces the secret of the Incarnation that was hidden from the people. This is why the hostile Nazarenes could taunt, "Is not this the carpenter's son?" The title of foster father, of course, has been used to guarantee that no one would doubt the virgin birth, but is Joseph's fatherhood limited to this?

It must be stated that, except for carnal generation, Joseph's role of father is much deeper, much more real. In our days, the Christian doctrine of the divine paternity is clearly understood by the faithful and known, though ridiculed, by unbelievers. We do not necessarily need to spend any time exploring that. It is, however, expedient for us to probe beyond that, to explore and extol the genuine, *unique* sense of Joseph's earthly paternity.

How is Joseph the father of Jesus? How is God's Son also Joseph's Son?

Let us note that besides calling Joseph "just," sacred Scripture also calls him father and does so without qualification. "Thy father and I have sought Thee sorrowing," Mary declares in Luke 2:48. Just a few verses before, Luke refers to Jesus' parents in 2:41-44, and implies parental authority in 2:51: "And He went down with

them and came to Nazareth, and was subject
to them."

By natural law, Jesus was subject to them
in His human nature, but not of course, in His
divinity. Indeed, in all scriptural references,
Joseph is head of the Holy Family and first in
authority. This was God's mission to him and, as
always, he obeyed, but this unheard of authority
(to command God!) was the source of Joseph's
humility. He knew better than anyone that
in this family, he was the least in sanctity and
dignity. All the faithful, in turn, recognize with
awe that, next to Mary, Joseph is the greatest
and most glorious of the saints. He shows us
how "the humble shall be exalted."[6]

Mary was Joseph's true wife. Joseph
freely consented to be her virginal husband.[ii]
Therefore, he is the virginal father of any fruit
produced of this virginal marriage. His was a
miraculous fatherhood. St. Augustine calls him
"Virgin Father of Jesus." Fr. Filas discusses the
meaning of fatherhood, demonstrating that it is

[ii]   It is from this that we get the term "Josephite marriage."
      Such a marriage is one where the spouses, generally for
      spiritual purposes, agree to live chastely and not have
      recourse to the marital act. Bl. Louis and Zélie Martin,
      the parents of St. Thérèse of Lisieux, lived this way for the
      first 10 months of their marriage, and Bl. Luigi and Maria
      Beltrame Quattrocchi did the same for the last 20 years of
      their married life.

essentially rooted in the intellect and will, that is, in knowing and loving.[7]

Joseph also assumed the paternal obligation to continue the work he began, to support, educate, cherish, and protect. There is a moral and spiritual bond between father and son, which is the ordinary consequence of generation, but which is also present in adoptive fathers. Joseph possessed this bond to the highest degree, but he should not be called an adoptive father. "Jesus is not alien to this family."[8]

St. Cyril of Jerusalem says:

> For just as Mary is called the mother of John [cf. John 19:26-27] because of love and not because she gave him birth, so Joseph is called father of Christ not by reason of generation, but by reason of the care he expended in supporting and rearing Him.[9]

In summary, Joseph is the earthly representative of the eternal, heavenly Father. St. Paul speaks of "the Father of Our Lord Jesus Christ, from whom all fatherhood in heaven and on earth receives its name."[10] Earthly fathers are reflections of the heavenly Father. In this regard, then, the paternity of Joseph is the supreme and most perfect mirror of God the Father. Moreover, like the Divine Father, Joseph's fatherhood is not by sexual union.

Rather, it is spiritual and virginal. In the Holy Trinity, the eternal generation of the Son is spiritual and not carnal. In the Incarnation, the conception of the Word made flesh is virginal and supernatural, even as concerns Mary, and is attributed in sacred Scripture and in the Creed not to the Father but to the Holy Spirit.

Yet unlike God the Father, Joseph's paternity is not in nature. This is an infinite difference. The two paternities cannot be equated, and our comparison in no way suggests this. When all is said and done, Joseph's title of earthly father is totally unique.

The Presentation

In Luke 2:27, 40 days after the birth of Jesus, it reads, "His parents brought in the child Jesus" to the Temple. After the event of the consecration, where Simeon and Anna both prophesy about Jesus, Luke concludes his account by noting, "his father and mother were marveling at the things which were spoken concerning Him." St. Luke will use the same language after the finding of the Child in the Temple.[11]

Joseph's role is silent here, but he is nonetheless present and active as a father. It is Mary who engages in the prophetic dialogue to which he stands as witness. Mary dominates

Luke's mind because he wishes to highlight her significance as Ark of the Covenant, and because, even though all pure, she obediently submits to the rite of legal purification.

Thinking of these parents, we observe with poignancy that theirs is the offering of the poor. While wealthier parents would have offered a lamb and a dove, they present five silver shekels to redeem their Son, the Redeemer of the world, by the sacrifice of two turtledoves or pigeons. Then Luke's quoting of Simeon, alluding as he does in priestly and sacrificial terms, prophetically indicates Christ's redemptive sacrifice.

In his magnificent book, *Our Father's Plan*,[12] Fr. William Most sees the event of the Presentation as the offertory of the priest/victim that will be consummated years later in the eucharistic consecration and sacrifice, which is one with the cross.

The Adoration of the Magi

St. Matthew tells us of the next episodes. When the exotic Magi (i.e., wise men) approached Bethlehem, the guiding star stands over the Holy Family's abode. We should note this interesting twist of vocabulary. Ancient tradition (St. Justin Martyr, for example) holds they were still in the stable/cave, since

the Greek word Matthew uses for "house" in
Gospel passage—*oikeia*—could be rendered in
the general sense of dwelling place.[iii] Yet it may
well be that Joseph in his solicitude had by this
time found a more suitable residence, perhaps
through connections with kin or friends.

However, it may also be that considerable
time, perhaps years had elapsed since Christmas.
We see a suggestion of this in that Herod, in
Matthew's account of the massacre of the Holy
Innocents, ordered the slaughter of all male
children two years of age and younger.[13]

Whatever the case may be, it would have
been Joseph as head of the household, who, in
his culture's norms of hospitality, would have
greeted the distinguished guests and ushered
them into the dwelling place where "they found
the Child with Mary His mother."[14]

The Flight into Egypt

Once more the type of the other Joseph,
son of Jacob, is evoked. Our Joseph again has a
dream. The angel tells him:

> Arise, and take the Child and His mother,
> and flee into Egypt, and remain there until
> I tell thee. For Herod will seek the Child to

[iii] This Greek word has the sense of not only house, but of
something domestic, something that is properly one's own,
which feeds into Father's analysis.

destroy Him. So he arose, and took the Child
and His mother by night and withdrew into
Egypt."[15]

As always, we see the decisive, immediate
obedience of Joseph to such a wrenching,
sacrificial action. Without any hesitation, he
pulls up roots and heads into the unknown.
Like his namesake, he goes into exile in Egypt,
a pagan land. As a "just" man, however, what
else could he do? Once he learned the will of
God, there could be no human calculation, and
so the protector of mother and Child embarked
once more on a journey of faith.

Various sites in Egypt lay claim to residence
by the Holy Family. Perhaps the presence of
a small Jewish colony might have attracted
them. If one refers to the historical record of
Herod's death, the exile lasted about three years.
Again, we must speculate about these strangers
transplanted into heathen territory with heathen
customs and culture. Even if some Jews had
settled there, Joseph would have had to make
shrewd adjustments in his trade as carpenter.
Supplies and demands were equally novel.
He must have used courtesy, industry, and
inventiveness to win a new clientele. To succeed,
he would have needed to win the admiration
and confidence of the native population.

After this extended exile, another dream

and an angel's voice once more summoned them to return. A new Exodus began. Herod, who had sought the life of the Child, was dead, but his son Archelaus ruled in his stead. Joseph had planned to reside in Bethlehem, it seems, but prudence prevailed. Archelaus, hardly less ruthless than his father, was also a threat. Therefore, the Holy Family traveled north to Nazareth, completing the circle begun in the first Advent.[iv]

[iv] Based on Josephus' *Antiquities of the Jews*, most historians believe Herod died in 4 BC, between March and early April. His final illness was excruciatingly painful, and it is speculated he had kidney disease. This is interesting because, as was noted in Fr. Gilsdorf's previous book *The Signs of the Times: Understanding the Church since Vatican II*, "The Jews thought the rein—or kidneys (*kilyah* in Hebrew)—was the seat of passion and the innermost being." If Herod had died of such a disease, it would have been fitting, given as he was to being ruled by his passions and not by God. His final illness was also marked by visible worms and putrefaction. His grandson Herod Agrippa died of similar symptoms.

Josephus tells us Herod was so worried no one would mourn at his death, he had all the kingdom's great, honorable men massacred so that at least someone would wail when he passed.

Before ascending the throne, Archelaus had roughly 3,000 Pharisees slain for sedition. Because he married his brother's widow (while his own wife was still alive), the Jews complained about this flagrant abuse of Mosaic law to Caesar Augustus. He was therefore deposed in 6 AD and exiled to what is now Vienne, France. He is said to have died around 18 AD.

The Finding in the Temple

Years later in Nazareth, Joseph escorts Mary and his 12-year-old Son on pilgrimage to the Temple. Once more, the Holy Family fulfills the Law of Moses. Since Jesus is now 12, He is obliged as a Son of the Covenant to undertake all the practices enjoined by the Law, including the Temple pilgrimages.

Here, too, Joseph carries out his mission as an earthly father of a heavenly Son. The pilgrims had the custom of traveling in separate companies, the men with the men, the women with the women. As an adult under the Law, Jesus could have been with Joseph and the men. On the other hand, since He was just over the cusp of being a child, He could have been with His mother in the women's company. Hence, His absence would not have been detected until the evening camp when families came together.

In pain, Mary and Joseph traveled through the night back to the Holy City. What words and prayers transpired between them in that dark, grief-stricken journey? This is a mystery both of sorrow and of joy, of incomprehension and wonderment.

Joseph's guiding presence is mentioned, but once more, no word of his is recorded. Instead, Mary addresses their Son for him. The parents are presented with an exceptional episode that interrupts the normalcy and quiet of their lives. What happens mystifies them (as we see by the fact that they are astonished). Jesus declares on this occasion the necessity of His being about His "Father's business." What Jesus has done, what they have suffered, the mysterious words of her Son's response—Mary guards all these things in her heart.[16] We can be sure Joseph does the same.

The episode ends with the treasured words, "the Child went back with them to Nazareth and was subject to them."[17] Joseph the humble obedient servant accepted with awe the obedience of the Son of God, Who was from then on known as "the carpenter's son."

STUDY QUESTIONS:

1. *In what sense can we call Joseph a father?*

2. *Fr. Gilsdorf claims, "Except for carnal generation, Joseph's role of father is much deeper, much more real." How so?*

3.   *What does Our Lord's submission to Joseph's authority reveal about the importance of obedience to godly authority? For help with this, see the Catechism of the Catholic Church 532, Luke 2:51-52, Luke 22:42, and Rom 13:1-2.*

4.   *If you are a parent, think of a time when you momentarily could not find your child, say in a grocery or department store or another public place. Think back to the panic you felt. Now put yourself in the place of Mary and Joseph as they looked for their "lost" Son. What range of emotions and thoughts do you think went through their heads?*

CHAPTER SEVEN

THE EARTHLY TRINITY

After the episode at the Temple, a discreet veil shrouds the Holy Family's lives. Except in a few general phrases of identification, Joseph will not be mentioned. We know Jesus lived in this home until His thirtieth year. We will return to this astounding mystery of the hidden life later, but for now let us focus on the Holy Family of Jesus, Mary, and Joseph.

We have already mentioned Leo XIII's encyclical *Quamquam Pluries*, which shows how Joseph fulfills the type of the Old Testament patriarch.

Pope Leo reminds us here that the Church is the family of God.[1] From this image, he then leads us to recognize that the kernel, the seed of the Church is already found in the communion of the Holy Family. Here the infant Church is represented: Jesus, its divine Founder, Mary, "Mother of the Church," and Joseph. Joseph continues to do for the Church of all times

what he did for his family during those years in
Bethlehem, Egypt, and Nazareth.

- He provided by the industry of his
  hands.
- He governed the household with
  humble prudence.[i]
- Oblivious of his own advantage,
  he cherished Jesus and Mary and
  sacrificed for them.
- He protected and defended the
  sacred persons of Jesus and Mary
  with constant vigilance, instant
  response, and courageous action,
  with utter disregard for his own
  inclinations and safety.

These, then, are the missions Joseph
accomplished daily at Nazareth. The following,
then, are those he fulfills daily for the Church:

---

[i]   This role requires some clarification. Pope Leo carefully
     says that Joseph governed "as with paternal authority,"
     analogous to that of a natural father by physical generation.
     Authority over Jesus was not jurisdiction in the strictest
     sense, although by natural law, Jesus was subject in His
     human nature to parental obedience; in this He freely
     submitted. This exercise of governing demonstrates the
     virtue of Joseph at its heights. As we commented earlier,
     the humility of Joseph knowing the divinity of Jesus and
     the surpassing holiness of Mary, in his obedience to his
     mission in perfect prudence, proves for us the deepest
     meaning of the description of "just man."

- He provides for us, thus preserving the Eucharist for our souls' nourishment and answering the prayers of the faithful with powerful intercession.

- He governs us, for Christ has made him "Lord of His house and ruler of His possessions."

- He cherishes all of us, as he loved Jesus and Mary.

- He protects us, for one of his greatest titles is "Protector and Defender of Holy Mother Church."[ii] As he assiduously guarded the body of Jesus, he now guards the Mystical Body of Christ, the Church.

To appreciate the position of Joseph within the Holy Family, we must keep in mind the two-fold foundation on which his privileges and duties rest, marriage and fatherhood, again

---

[ii] Bl. Pius IX gave him this title in *Quemadmodum Deus*, a decree issued on December 8, 1870, by the Sacred Congregation of Rites. According to Fr. Blaine Burkey, OFM Cap, this was done because the Papal States had recently been dissolved by the new Italian government and the Pope made a "prisoner of the Vatican." December 8 was declared a national day of prayer for the Pope. Thus *QD* was released that day in conjunction with this event. Leo XIII reaffirmed this designation in *Quamquam Pluries*. This latter Pontiff also approved the St. Joseph Scapular.

remembering he is true husband of Mary and true father of Jesus.

As we have seen, the skeptical and hostile in the Gospels refer to Jesus as the carpenter's son. These same critics say they know His mother and brethren. Ironically, their very boast shows they know nothing of the secret of this family. The divine purpose has been perfectly attained; the mystery of the Incarnation has remained hidden until the time set for its revelation.

This principle of normalcy assures us that on the surface, life in the Holy Family's humble dwelling was routine and ordinary. They saw Mary at the well and around the house. They saw Jesus as He grew from boy to man on the village's streets, in the fields at play with companions, at work, and always in the synagogue at prayer and instruction. They saw Joseph going out to meet customers and get supplies. After delivering his products, he would return, not with coins, but with goods received in barter. Perhaps Jesus went along to assist him. Everyone recognized that Joseph was a just man.

The townsfolk observed all these ordinary, mundane things, but what they could not have known was that, in reality, this quiet home was the beachhead for the reconquest of the world from the enemy, the hinge of all history, the womb of the Church.

Joseph the Worker

Earlier we discussed the Gospel information on Joseph's trade. We saw evidence that he was indeed a carpenter who worked in wood. Fr. Filas observes that at Nazareth, the curse of Genesis, "By the sweat of your face shall you eat your bread,"[2] has become for us one of the greatest blessings exemplified most perfectly in Joseph.[3]

It is then most fitting that in 1920, Pope Benedict XV declared by *motu proprio* Joseph as "Patron of Workers."[4] (Even before this, of course, the Church had related Joseph to workers in a less formal way.) Also fitting is that on May 1, 1955, Pope Pius XII instituted the Feast of St. Joseph the Worker as a response to the challenge of communism's May Day appeal to the proletariat.[iii]

[iii] The Servant of God Pius XII did this in an address to the Catholic Association of Italian Workers, whose aim was to promote a genuine culture of respect for laborers' rights against the counterfeit respect given by the communists. It is hard even for those of us who lived through the height of communism to remember the pull this atheistic, materialistic ideology had on many workers. Each year communist nations and movements in non-communist nations held their celebration of labor on May 1 (which even many Western nations commemorate as Labor Day). By proclaiming this day as the Feast of St. Joseph the Worker, Pius attempted to show St. Joseph (and, by extension, the Church) identified with and supported the legitimate aspirations of the working class to fair wages, just

What is most fascinating is that from early boyhood, Jesus was at the workbench alongside Joseph. Though He possessed full intellectual understanding as a Divine Person, He humbly willed to acquire an experimental, hands-on habit and art of the trade under Joseph's tutelage.

Throughout these blessed years, father and Son worked as a team. What happened on any given day? What words passed between the two of them? What were the signs of love, of humor, of affection and concern, of prayer? Pope Pius IX comes to our aid in *Quemadmodum Deus*:

> And so it was that Him whom countless kings and prophets had of old desired to see, Joseph not only saw but conversed with, and embraced in paternal affection, and kissed, and most diligently reared—even Him whom the faithful were to receive in the bread that came down from heaven whereby they might obtain eternal life.[5]

The Holy Family

It has been aptly remarked that no one else but Joseph lived with Jesus and Mary in the

---

treatment, and the upholding of the inherent dignity of all workers. He told them, "You have beside you a shepherd, a defender, and a father" in St. Joseph.

Holy Family, to whom Pope Leo XIII strongly promoted devotion. Among other acts, he issued an apostolic brief on the subject, *Neminem Fugit*. He wrote:

> When God in His mercy decided to carry out the work of man's redemption, so long expected through the centuries, He arranged to perform His task in such a way that in its beginnings it might show forth to the world the august spectacle of a divinely founded family. In this, all men were to behold the perfect exemplar of domestic society, as well as of all virtue and holiness.[6]

Such indeed was the family of Nazareth. In its bosom was concealed the Sun of Justice, awaiting in anticipation the time when His full splendors should shine on all the nations—Christ our God, our Savior, together with His Virgin Mother and Joseph, that most blessed man who exercised the rights of father over Jesus.

We cannot doubt, then, that all the glories of the domestic life, taking their origin in mutual charity, saintly character, and the exercise of piety, were without exception manifested in a superlative degree by the Holy Family, in order that all Christians in whatever walk of life or situation might have a reason and an incentive to practice every virtue, provided they would fix their gaze on the Holy Family. Therefore, in Joseph heads of the household are blessed with the unsurpassed model of fatherly watchfulness and care.

After beautiful reference to Mary and Jesus and applications to various states of life, Pope Leo addressed workers, calling upon them to recognize their common lot with the Holy Family:

> Joseph, too, was bound to find ways and means of wresting a livelihood out of his earnings, while the very hands of God plied the tools of a carpenter.[7]

In an extraordinary and touching Lenten message to American schoolchildren, Pope Pius XII told them of St. Joseph in very simple childlike language:

> Day after day, at home and in the carpenter's shop, his eyes rested on Jesus; he protected Him against the dangers of childhood; he guided His advancing years, and by hard work and with religious devotedness he provided for the increasing needs of the Mother and the Son.... And there was Joseph, modest, self-effacing, yet exercising authority over that family. How holy he must have been! Under his fatherly protection and ceaseless, tireless care the young Boy grew into manhood....

Don't you think that now in heaven he is
the same loving father and guardian of the
whole Church, of all its members, as he was
of its Head on earth? We hear your answer:
Yes. And does he not know that oh so many
of its children are terribly in need of help?
They need help for their souls—the grace of
repentance, the grace of humble, unstinted
surrender to the holy will of God; and Joseph
turns to Jesus, of old his Boy of Nazareth and
at once graces flow abundantly for the souls
of men."[8]

Joseph has been inserted into the mystery
of the Incarnation. As far as can be known,
the Holy Family was first called "the earthly
Trinity" by Walahfrid Strabo.[iv] This exalted
title has been echoed ever since. Pope John
Paul II once reminded us that every family is
a "reflection of the Trinity."[9] How much more
true is this of the Holy Family? It follows,
therefore, that every family can only reflect the
Trinity by imitating the family of Nazareth.
In this family communion, Joseph was in
union with the Holiest, gave Him His earthly

[iv] Strabo was an early ninth century Benedictine monk,
botanist, educator, diplomat, and poet. Indeed, he was one
of the most important poets of the Carolingian Renaissance,
and he wrote a work that many consider a worthy precursor
of Dante's *Divine Comedy*, in which Strabo placed even
luminaries such as Charlemagne in hell.

name, and commanded God as his own Son on
Earth.

We might well contrast God's plan for this
family with what we might have schemed.
How would we have arranged the economy
of the Holy Family? Perhaps we would have
had Hollywood or the television networks
orchestrate a gala reception with full coverage
of the first days. We would have conducted a
fund drive to settle them comfortably in a grand
palace. But soon after all this, who would have
continued to pay heed or, even less, surrender
their hearts to them or seek to draw from them
any lessons for salvation?

As we read in Isaiah 55:8-9:

> For My thoughts are not your thoughts,
> nor are My ways your ways. For as far as the
> heavens are above the earth, so are My ways
> above your ways, and My thoughts above
> your thoughts.

The Church has never explicitly defined
anything concerning St. Joseph exclusively.
But references in Scripture offer a solid base
from which the Fathers, saints, popes, and
theologians have elaborated sound, edifying,
and prudent commentaries on his exalted (albeit
shrouded) position, most of which are logically
deduced from Joseph's vocation. From two

biblical patterns, we can discern and appreciate his vocation and mission:

1. God gives all necessary preparations and dispositions to those whom He calls to exalted missions. The prime example of this fact is Mary.

2. God enlightens those He calls in a manner sufficient for them to understand and carry out the mission. As the saying goes, "He doesn't call the equipped, He equips the called."

The application of these patterns to Joseph is obvious and justified.

Beyond the common teachings on the man that we have previously discussed, some have raised further speculations, including whether Joseph himself was immaculately conceived. Theologians, however, no longer accept this. Indeed, Pope Pius XII says Mary is unique in this privilege, which was "never granted to anyone else."[10]

But was Joseph granted sanctification in the womb (as theologians speculate happened with John the Baptist, based on Luke 1:44)? This and the theory of his bodily assumption must remain in the realm of mere speculation.[v]

---

[v] Militating against an assumption of Joseph after his death is that, unlike the Blessed Virgin, we have relics of the

Incidentally, the Gospel passages in which Jesus attributes the primacy of greatness to John the Baptist[11] in no way detracts from the primacy of Joseph, second only to Mary, since Joseph, as Mary, already stands in the new order of the Incarnation. Rather, Christ is speaking here in the style of Semitic hyperbole assessing the role of His precursor in the light of the former dispensation.

We might also speak of the heart of Joseph. The biblical theology of the heart, so solidly established in the life of the Church, is the source of Catholic devotion to the Sacred Heart of Jesus and the Immaculate Heart of Mary. Should we extend this devotion to the heart of Joseph? The Church has not approved this as part of her public devotion, and she stated so in a decree of June 14, 1873.[12] Yet privately, we can profit by a silent contemplation of the heart of this pure and courageous guardian. After all, the Immaculate Heart of Mary loved his heart as that of her husband. The Sacred Heart of Jesus loved his heart as that of His father. If then we unite our hearts with those of Jesus and Mary,

---

"Guardian of the Redeemer," as John Paul II called him in his apostolic exhortation *Redemptoris Custos*. Indeed, among others in its collection, the Bulgarian National History Museum has a relic of him that was attested to as authentic in 1770 and 1772 by Bishop Nicola Angelo Maria Landini, then-perfect of the Vatican reliquary.

as the Church urges us to do, should we not also be moved to imitate their love for the heart of Joseph, the third person of the earthly Trinity?

STUDY QUESTIONS:

1. *Fr. Gilsdorf calls the Holy Family the "earthly Trinity." How are the heavenly Trinity and the "earthly Trinity" similar? How are they different? How is the Church like both?*

2. *Judging by Father's description of the Holy Family, what is God's vision for all families? How is that different from society's? How is that different from your own? Does your vision of the family more closely align with God's or society's? What would have to happen to make your vision more like that of God?*

3.   *What was Joseph's role in the Holy Family?*

4.   *What was the two-fold foundation on which Joseph's privileges and duties within the Holy Family rested?*

CHAPTER EIGHT

PATRON AND PATRIARCH

Some time before the Christ began His public ministry, Joseph died. When he did, tradition and the logic of Christian hearts tell us he breathed his last in the arms of Jesus and Mary. The second greatest saint—only Mary surpasses him—entered peacefully into eternity with his hands filled with merit.

Since it is screened behind the silence of Scripture, it would be rash to presume to describe the scene. Nonetheless, one can well imagine the Holy Family's last moments together, the intense emotion of love, the enlightened vision of the glory that awaited him, the certainty of eternal rest and perpetual light that gave consolation to the wife and the Son, but also the human sorrow. After all, Christ wept at the tomb of Lazarus, and witnesses said, "See how He loved him!" He wept at other times, too, as when He cried over the future of Jerusalem.[1] How much more would He have shed tears over the passing of His father?

I picture Joseph's eyes radiating with joy as he gazed upon his family for the last time in this world. In a relatively short span of time, they would be reunited in the beatific vision of the heavenly Trinity. For these reasons, Joseph is named the patron of a happy death, and for these same reasons his death and that of those devoted to him is called happy. We should daily repeat with fervor the beautiful traditional invocation:

> Jesus, Mary, and Joseph, I give you my heart and my soul!
> Jesus, Mary, and Joseph, assist me in my last agony!
> Jesus, Mary, and Joseph, may I breathe forth my soul in peace with you! Amen.

His patronage and titles extend to countless other areas as well.

- Patron of the universal Church [2][i]
- Head of the Holy Family[3]
- Patron of workers[4]
- Defender against communism[5]

---

[i] We recall how this title was based on the concept of the Holy Family as the "seed" of the Church.

These are but a few of his titles. One need but review the beautiful Litany of St. Joseph to appreciate the range of his intercession.[ii]

We might suggest another unofficial title so meaningful in our day, that of patron of priests. St. Bernard was the author of an antiphon once used as a prayer of preparation before the celebration of Holy Mass. It read, "O fortunate man, blessed Joseph, to whom it was given to see the God whom many kings yearned to see and did not see, to hear the God whom many kings yearned to hear and did not hear; not only to see and hear, but to carry, to kiss, to clothe, and protect Him."

How appropriate that prayer is. It is echoed by Pope Pius IX in *Quemadmodum Deus*, and it is to be highly recommended to priests before the eucharistic sacrifice, for in a special way they share in the intimacy expressed in this prayer. As patriarch of the New Covenant, Joseph defended and preserved the Bread of Life from the moment of His first repose in the food trough of the stable. He did so in the House of Bread, Bethlehem. He did so in Egypt, the same place where the Joseph of Genesis was custodian and distributor of the grain. Daily, he nurtured and supported the True Manna come down from heaven. He was granted an

---

[ii] See Appendix 2.

intimacy shared only by Mary. Today, we can go pray before the Real Presence, but he *lived* in the Real Presence of Jesus and was absorbed in an atmosphere of contemplative prayer.

Moreover, he lived a life of chastity and virginity, as was required of his vocation from youth. It is obvious, therefore, why priests, who are custodians of the Eucharist, should foster a personal devotion in their vocation to Joseph, especially at a time like our own when devotion to the Blessed Sacrament is drastically diminished, a time when the Eucharist literally needs priestly protection. Ours is also a time when contentious voices are questioning the discipline of priestly celibacy, and when prayer is seldom seen as a direct contemplative communication between God and the soul. Yet Joseph, again, was a protector, he was chaste, he was prayerful.

One more bond attaches the priest to Joseph. On Calvary, the beloved and youngest disciple St. John received from Jesus as a priceless inheritance the care and custody of His mother. From that time, John took her into his home. John, a newly ordained priest, assumed the role Joseph had carried out so faithfully until his death, a role Jesus had supplied until the moment of His death, and which every priest assumes as a joyful glory of his ministry.

STUDY QUESTIONS:

1. *Looking at Joseph's life, of what other things might we consider him patron?*

2. *Why might the Church call St. Joseph "patron of a happy death"? For some additional background, read the Catechism 1014.*

3. *We do not often think of Jesus as having human emotions, and yet we know from the Bible that He cried on several occasions (cf., John 11:35, Luke 19:41). Thus, it is entirely conceivable that He wept at Joseph's death. What sort of memories do you think came flooding back to Him? In what ways do you think Jesus missed Joseph afterward?*

4. *Of course, some people's experience of their fathers is not so positive. How can meditating on Joseph's fatherhood be a source of healing and grace for people in this position?*

5. *What sort of role model is Joseph for today's priests?*

CHAPTER NINE

THE MYSTERY OF SILENCE

One of the most striking, perplexing, and largely unknown facts about St. Joseph is that devotion to this second greatest saint was muted and minimal until the Middle Ages.[i]

As we saw earlier, the six major apocryphal accounts that purport to give details of his life contain so much confusion, error, and even heresy that it tainted the image people (especially the common faithful) had of Joseph. Other writers only added to this problem. As a result, many of the legends about him endured even into our own age (even though occasional efforts were made to separate truth from fiction).

Apart from the stories, however, there were other popular manifestations of devotion to the last Patriarch. For instance, we do know of a

---

[i] For a detailed history of devotion to St. Joseph, we refer the reader to the works of Fr. Filas listed in the bibliography. What follows is a brief summary gleaned from the extensive factual information from these most valuable sources.

painted image of him from the third century
and of a church erected in his honor by St.
Helena at Nazareth in the fourth. In the eastern
regions of the Church, theological study of St.
Joseph did not develop much beyond Sts. Basil,
Gregory of Nyssa, and Gregory Nazianzus.
In the West, the writings of St. Augustine,
St. Jerome the Venerable, the aforementioned
Walahfrid Strabo, and others promoted the
first liturgical recognition of St. Joseph in the
martyrologies read during the Divine Office in
the monasteries of Europe.

For instance, Strabo penned this magnificent
praise:

> The shepherds found Mary, Joseph, and the
> Child; through these three, the world was
> healed.[1]

In Egypt, some attention was given to the
Holy Family but not specifically to Joseph. However, by the seventh century, the Coptic Christians had established a feast in his honor on July
20, and by the tenth century, a number of other
calendars also featured a Feast of St. Joseph.

The cradle of the sort of devotion we see
today, however, was the monastery of St. Sabas
in Palestine, from which a feast dedicated to
this holiest of men spread slowly from about
the year 1000.

The year 1480 marked a major advance of devotion to Joseph in the liturgy, for in 1479, Pope Sixtus IV (1471–1484) had instituted the Feast of St. Joseph in the Church in Rome, whence it quickly spread through Italy and beyond.[ii]

Coinciding with this was the creation of a liturgical canon for the feast that has come down to our own day:

> To Gabriel alone in heaven and to thee alone, O highly praised and blessed Joseph, after the Virgin only was the all-unique and fearsome mystery confided which hurled back the corrupter and prince of darkness.[2]

A major contribution to the devotion this saint enjoys was made by St. Bernard of Clairvaux, first by virtue of the antiphon cited in our last chapter and probably more importantly his masterful comparison of Joseph of Egypt with Joseph of Nazareth. Earlier Fathers had connected the two, albeit without developing the reasons. Theological debates during the Middle Ages also helped to clarify the image of St. Joseph.

One of his greatest promoters was John Gerson, chancellor of the University of Paris,[iii]

[ii] It was by mere coincidence and error, too complicated to discuss here, that March 19 was chosen as the official day of commemoration, and even then that date only gradually became universal.

[iii] Jean Gerson (1363–1429) gave sermons in which he

who used his influence at the highest levels
to establish a more universal feast. For this
purpose, he composed "The Josephina" and
"Considerations on St. Joseph," and delivered
the sermon for the Feast of the Nativity of Mary,
September 8, 1416, to the Fathers of the Council
of Constance.[iv] He urged an official invocation
of St. Joseph and his institution feast in order
to restore unity to the Church (then divided
grievously by the Great Western Schism). He
said the main principle in the theology of Joseph
was the fact that he was the true husband of the
mother of God the Son. From this one crucial
point, Gerson derived all his conclusions on
Joseph's dignity and holiness. Since being her
spouse was his election and vocation, and since
this came directly from God, it follows that

---

glorified St. Joseph, and wrote *Les Considérations sur saint
Joseph* and a long poem of 4,800 verses, the *Josephina*.
According to Gerson, Joseph was a young man at his
wedding. He believed Joseph was sanctified in the womb
of his mother (just like John the Baptist), and he believed
his bodily assumption was possible.

[iv] The Church's sixteenth ecumenical council (1414–1418).
By declaring Martin V as pontiff, it resolved the "Great
Western Schism" (which occurred when three men claimed
the papacy, thus splitting the Western Church into rival
factions). It also condemned Jan Hus, the Czech heretic,
and helped develop the Church's teaching on national
sovereignty, freedom of conscience in religion, and the just
war theory. It was the zenith for the movement that was
later called the heresy of "conciliarism," which teaches the
power of Councils exceeds that of popes.

Joseph was endowed with all the privileges and virtues pertaining to his office.

Pierre Cardinal d'Ailly,[v] a close friend and former teacher, was inspired by Gerson to write his tractate on the 12 prerogatives of St. Joseph, and this work spread rapidly upon its completion. Another contemporary promoter of devotion to Joseph was the great Franciscan preacher St. Bernadine of Siena, who died in 1444 AD.[vi]

---

[v] According to the *Catholic Encyclopedia*, d'Ailly was a "French theologian and philosopher, bishop and cardinal, born 1350 at Compiègne; died probably 1420 at Avignon. He studied at the College of Navarre, University of Paris.... In 1384 he became director of the College of Navarre; Gerson and Nicholas of Clemanges were among his pupils.... [He was later] made Chancellor of the University, Confessor of the King, and Treasurer of the Sainte Chapelle." He was an extreme conciliarist and was also a nominalist. (According to George Weigel, nominalism was "a powerful late-medieval philosophical movement that denied that universal concepts and principles exist in reality—they exist only in our minds. According to the nominalists, there is, to take an obvious and critical example, no such thing as 'human nature' per se. 'Human nature' is simply a description, a name (hence 'nominalism') we give to our experience of common features among human beings. The only things that exist, according to nominalism, are particulars.") Additionally, he was an astronomer who believed the East Indies could be reached by sailing West (and thus had a profound influence upon Columbus), and his astronomical work helped spark the reform which led to the current Gregorian calendar.

[vi] Italian Franciscan missionary whose preaching helped foment the fifteenth century's religious revival. He is also

Alongside these more learned contributions, popular and devotional literature also treated of the saint. In these works, Christians saw the need to bind Joseph with Mary in their devotions. Unfortunately, these writings were largely influenced by the apocrypha, whose legends the common faithful gradually absorbed. Hence, from this period we find some bizarre and erroneous elements. These in turn contaminated the famous miracle plays of the twelfth and thirteenth centuries.

Despite the incorrect information they helped popularize, the earlier plays at least stimulated recognition of Joseph and his role. The same is true of religious art, which reflected the apocrypha as we can see through the images that have endured to our own times (e.g., the blossoming staff of Joseph and his exaggerated age).

Then in the early sixteenth century, the

---

credited with helping to foster devotion to the Holy Name of Jesus. His indefatigable missionary efforts were largely responsible for so many Greeks attending the Council of Florence (1431–45), which briefly saw the Eastern and Western Churches reunited. Some believe the inroads made by Protestantism in Europe would have been much worse were it not for the fact that many monastic orders copied his example of widespread preaching outside of the Mass.

Italian Capuchin John of Fano[vii] introduced devotion to the Seven Sorrows of St. Joseph.[viii]

As a side effect of the Council of Trent, devotion to Joseph began to flourish in the religious orders after 1550. It was spearheaded by the newly founded Jesuits of St. Ignatius, as well as by St. Teresa of Avila among the Carmelites. The great Teresa remarked that "as Joseph commanded on earth, so it seems he does in heaven.... [His Son] never failed to answer his prayers." Teresa spoke of Joseph as "my advocate master."[3]

Soon St. Joseph was chosen by Catholics of both the Old and New Worlds as their patron.

[vii] Born in 1469, Giovanni da Fano joined the Observant Franciscans around 1485. Ordained in 1492, he became an itinerant preacher (he was especially effective preaching against Lutheranism), and was later named Minister General of his Franciscan province. When two men of his Order began the Capuchin reform, he initially tried to thwart their efforts, but eventually ended up joining them. He died on March 5, 1539, while preaching a Lenten mission in Urbania.

[viii] The Seven Sorrows of St. Joseph are: 1) Finding Our Lady had conceived and believing that his only option was to "put her away;" 2) Not finding lodging in the city of Bethlehem; 3) Seeing the Divine Infant suffer and shed blood at the Circumcision; 4) Hearing the prophecy of St. Simeon that Jesus would be an object of contradiction and that Mary's own soul would be pierced by a sword; 5) The Flight into Egypt; 6) When returning from Egypt, finding the cruel Archelaus had succeeded Herod the Great; 7) Losing the Child Jesus for three days.

Moreover, as we have already mentioned, Bl. Pius IX designated Joseph patron of the universal Church in 1870. Since then, popes have lavishly honored him, and their writings have soundly advanced the theological foundations of true devotion to the spouse of Mary.

Having mentioned the New World above, it will be of special interest to speak further of North America. St. Joseph is the patron saint of Canada, in part because the North American martyrs established a mission in St. Joseph's name among the Hurons.[ix] So also the first mission among the Algonquins was dedicated to his patronage, and other missionaries and explorers gave his name to islands and rivers around the continent. For example, the missionary and explorer Fr. Claude Allouez, SJ (1622-1689), dedicated what is now called Lake Michigan as Lake St. Joseph. Numerous churches were also consecrated in his name.

Furthermore, this phenomenon was not limited to Canada. Many places in the United States are honored to bear the name of the just man. St. Elizabeth Seton named her religious

---

[ix] Killed by Native Americans, the North American martyrs were the Jesuit priests St. Jean de Brébeuf, St. Noel Chabanel, St. Anthony Daniel, St. Charles Garnier, St. Isaac Joques, and St. Gabriel Lalemant, and the laymen St. Jean de la Lande and St. René Goupil (a surgeon who was also the first to be martyred on September 29, 1642).

order the Sisters of St. Joseph, and its motherhouse still bears his name. The strong devotion to Joseph that has been a feature of Catholic life in the United States is a testimony to his powerful intercession on behalf of his clients.

Of course, when discussing St. Joseph in the United States, we must mention the extraordinary miraculous stairway in Santa Fe, New Mexico.

In 1852, the Sisters of Loretto established a convent there and later opened a school. For this, the bishop commissioned a chapel, which was completed in 1878. A gross error, a comedy if it were not a tragedy, resulted in a magnificent chapel—with no access to the choir loft! Many experts were consulted, and their verdict was that it would be useless to install stairs since nothing would be gained. Doing so, they said, would take up far too much room, and it would add no seating space (which was the loft's original purpose). The sisters made a novena to St. Joseph.

On the ninth day, a gray-haired man appeared at the door with a saddled burro and bearing an ancient toolbox. He asked if the sisters had any carpentry work, and when they showed him what was needed, he offered to solve the problem of the stairway on condition that no one would enter the chapel while he worked.

After three months, he asked the Sister Superior to inspect his creation of a spiral staircase with two complete 360-degree turns. When all the sisters were called in, the old man disappeared. The old man had no supply of wood when he arrived. There was no record of local sale of wood. Moreover, the wood used was not native to the area. The exquisite staircase of 33 steps has no central support. Engineers testify that with his equipment—a T-square, hammer, antique saw, and a chisel—it should have been impossible to accomplish this marvel of beauty and precision. The stairs still stand firm after a century of use.[x] By all known laws of physics, the structure should have collapsed the first time anyone dared to ascend. The sisters and

---

[x] The Loretto Chapel is now a for-profit museum that is rented out for weddings and such. Sadly, the staircase is closed. Furthermore, since Fr. Gilsdorf wrote this, evidence has surfaced to suggest the carpenter was François-Jean Rochas, a member of an order of celibate tradesmen who was later murdered. Tending to confirm this is an entry in the sisters' ledger from March 1881, found by local historian Mary Jean Straw Cook, which shows $150 was paid for wood to Mr. Rochas. However, as one online commentator has noted, "So, discovering that St. Joseph didn't build the spiral staircase, you'd think that would burst my bubble, wouldn't you? But it doesn't. He still had a direct hand in the project: When the sisters prayed for help, they prayed a novena to St. Joseph." Through his intercession, God sent the sisters the right man to do the job. And looking at the staircase's design, it does seem to have been divinely inspired.

faithful people have an idea about the identity of the itinerant master carpenter. This is but one of thousands of cases—some more, some less extraordinary—of the quiet but powerful aid of St. Joseph to those who call on him.[4]

All of North America turns with reverence toward the recently beatified Br. André Bessette, CSC.[xi] This humble man entered the Congregation of the Holy Cross as a lay brother and ranked among the least of his confreres. While excelling in all Catholic devotion, his consuming love for St. Joseph was truly the hallmark of his life. His main labor was inspiring and guiding the construction of the splendid Oratory of St. Joseph in Montreal. That a simple brother could initiate and follow through so thoroughly and magnificently with such a major undertaking was remarkable and providential.

Phenomenal miracles were worked through Bl. André, all credited to St. Joseph, and these demonstrated that his life was blessed by heavenly approval. There is a moving little book on his life that was in its fourth printing in 1969, *Brother André: The Wonder Man of Mount Royal.*[5] The full impact of this living image of St. Joseph can only be appreciated by a prayerful

---

[xi] The Servant of God John Paul II beatified Bl. André Bessette, CSC (1845–1937) on May 23, 1982.

study of his long life of 92 wondrous years. A pilgrimage to the oratory, now a basilica, would be an excellent place to start.

The role of St. Joseph in modern Marian apparitions bears a special message for our times. In 1879, a silent living tableau appeared on the wall of the parish church at Knock, Ireland. In it, Joseph stood flanking the Blessed Virgin and the Lamb of the Apocalypse, with St. John the Beloved Disciple on the opposite side (who, because he took Our Lady into his home, could be called the second Joseph). Joseph bends with humble obeisance toward Mary and the Lamb.

The apocalyptic theme of that apparition was greatly enhanced during the central apparition of the twentieth century at Fatima. In the final apparition on October 13, 1917, the occasion of the famed miracle of the sun, St. Joseph appeared holding the child Jesus in his arms and blessing the world as with a eucharistic monstrance. Mary had told the children in the previous apparition in September that, "St. Joseph will come with the Child Jesus to give peace to the world." There is a traditional belief by many holy souls that when the whole world finally and fully comprehends the sanctity and power of St. Joseph, the world will be saved.

By way of summary, we may be helped by

an outline suggested by Fr. Filas based on the four distinct periods of St. Joseph.[6]

- The first 500 years: St. Joseph was neglected due to pressures of dogmatic issues centering on the person of Jesus and the role of Mary Ever-Virgin Mother. This is the era of Christological controversies.
- From 500–1000 AD: Veneration begins to grow in the monasteries
- From 1000–1500 AD: Formal devotion to Joseph begins to spread, and a feast is instituted in his honor
- From the mid 1500s to the present: Joseph finally enters his glory on earth and in the Church.

This admittedly long discussion allows us to ask once more: Why the early obscurity?

In considering this question, we could also ask, why the obscurity in the Gospel accounts? What drove the sacred authors' reticence in saying so little about Joseph, with not one word of his being recorded? Granted, as noted just above, the early extra-biblical obscurity was deliberate and due to the great heresies concerning the person of Jesus and the hypostatic union of His two natures. These were the nascent Church's crucial challenges.

In addition, while the early Christians' doctrine could never separate Mary's virginity from these questions, they avoided highlighting Joseph's role in order to avoid doubts about the virgin birth. Thus, prudential and tactical reasons drove the early obscurity.

Furthermore, although Scripture is indeed largely silent about Joseph, this is not something unique. Consider the hidden life of Jesus and Mary. Even though Scripture speaks of the public ministry of Jesus, we wish we knew much more about Him. St. John the Evangelist says that if all the things Jesus said or did were put to paper, "the whole world could not hold the books that would be written."[7]

Certainly, we wish we had more information concerning our Blessed Mother. We also long to have more background in many other episodes in the Gospels. For instance, who were the young man and woman married at Cana? What was their relationship to Mary and Jesus that inspired the couple to invite them? What happened to them in the future regarding their family and in the community of the Church?

We must understand there is a reason the Holy Spirit in His infinite wisdom has told us only so much and no more. One obvious reason is that by limiting the information, all persons of all places and times can apply the basic facts to their own individual lives. The more additional details given, the harder it would be in meditation to apply such specific circumstances to one's own personal situation. Thus, families of all ages can more readily imitate the essential virtues of the Holy Family. Married couples can emulate the holy bond of Mary and Joseph and thereby discover guidance and blessings for their family life. They will also learn that this begins by doing what the spouses of Cana did: They must invite Jesus and Mary to be present at their weddings and in their homes. Young girls, wives, widows, virgins, and mothers can imitate Mary in those things which her Spouse the Holy Spirit has seen sufficient to reveal to us.

Joseph, the just man, can be an example for all the faithful, but he serves in a special way as a model for young men to answer God's challenge in all walks of life. He can be the strong patron and intercessor of workers and family providers. He can be a special patron of priests married to the Church in a virginal life, custodians of the Holy Eucharist, the Person of Jesus Christ, living daily in their midst for the life of the world.

Yes, we have many mysteries in our Faith, of which the hidden life cloaked in the silence of Scripture is one of the greatest and most

instructive. After all, divine mysteries are said
to be "ineffable," which means they go beyond
our human ability to express in words.

It is this silence that has prompted often
wretched attempts to fill in the gaps. We
understand but regret the concoctions of the
apocrypha. Other edifying and helpful sources
exist, however, that fulfill the same craving to
know more, provided we clearly understand
their nature and limits.

Thus the recorded visions of holy souls
often prove instructive, especially those of Mary
of Ágreda and Anne Catherine Emmerich. Now
we must never confuse or equate the authority
of the private revelations imparted to pious souls
with that of divine revelation (given to us in
Scripture and Tradition as interpreted for us by
the Magisterium of the Church). That is one
reason why in this short study we have mainly
chosen to restrict ourselves to sacred Scripture
and the conclusions we can derive from the
inspired text.

Still, we sometimes hear people say, "No,
that can't be true. We know much more than
that. Bl. Anne Catherine Emmerich said … etc."
This type of thinking would distort the genuine
value of the meditations of these favored friends
of God, as they themselves insisted.

Nevertheless, for edification and stimulus

for our own meditation, we should not hesitate to read these fully orthodox sources, provided we never equate them with holy Scripture or put more than human credence in the details they offer (which are not guaranteed) when they go beyond the data of the Gospels.

We might add that just as we have seen devotion to Mary eclipsed among many who have been beguiled by false interpretations of the Second Vatican Council, so an ever-deepening eclipse has shadowed devotion to her spouse, the second greatest saint. Such eclipses are but temporary though fearful phenomena. This, too, shall pass, and in the great triumph of Mary foretold at Fatima, knowledge and love for St. Joseph will burst forth in a fullness and splendor never before experienced. A world starving for the true Bread of everlasting Life will finally hear and answer the call: **Go to Joseph!**

STUDY QUESTIONS:

1. *How did devotion to St. Joseph develop? Either reread the first part of the chapter or simply review Fr. Filas' four periods of Josephite devotion.*

2. *Why was Joseph more obscure in the very early Church compared, say, to the Blessed Virgin?*

3. *Why do you suppose Strabo says, "Through these three, the world was healed"?*

4. *Why is the monastery of St. Sabas in Palestine important in the development of devotion to St. Joseph?*

5. How has Christianity been aided by the ever-increasing reflection over the centuries concerning St. Joseph and the role he played?

6. Go back and reread some of the ways that Joseph's intercession was responsible for obtaining graces or favors from the Lord. Is the Guardian of the Redeemer part of your prayer life? Why? If not, why not?

7. Would increased devotion to St. Joseph in our age help? If so, how?

8. Fr. Gilsdorf writes, "There is a reason the Holy Spirit in His infinite wisdom has told us only so much and no more." Why do you think this is? Why might He have kept so much about St. Joseph so hidden?

9.   *The ultimate purpose of devotion to any saint is to lead us closer to Jesus. How does devotion to St. Joseph accomplish this?*

10.   *Oftentimes, women find St. Joseph leaves them cold. "I'm not a husband. I'm not a father," they will say. "What does his life have to say to me?" How can the ultimate Patriarch and the role he played be more relevant to women and lead them closer to Jesus?*

SUGGESTED READINGS

Quemadmodum Deus, "As Almighty God," decree, Sacred Congregation of Rites, December 8, 1870

Quamquam Pluries, "On Devotion to St. Joseph," encyclical, Pope Leo XIII, August 15, 1889

Neminem Fugit, "Everyone Knows," apostolic letter, Leo XIII, June 14, 1892, AAS 12 (1892), p. 149f

Bonum Sane, "It is Good and Salutary," motu proprio, Benedict XV, July 25, 1920, AAS 12 (1920), pp. 313- 317

"Radio Message to Catholic School Students in the United States of America," Pius XII, February 19, 1958: AAS 50 (1958), p. 174

Novis hisce temporibus, decree adding St. Joseph to the Mass, Sacred Congregation of Rites, November 13, 1962: AAS 54 (1962), p. 873.12

Brother André: The Wonder Man of Mount Royal, by Henri-Paul Bergeron, CSC, translated by Real Boudreau, CSC (Montreal: Fides Publishers, 1958)

The Divine Life of the Most Holy Virgin: Being an Abridgement of the Mystical City of God, by Ven. Mary of Ágreda (Rockford, IL: TAN Books & Publishers, 1997)

The Life of the Blessed Virgin Mary, by Bl. Anne Catherine Emmerich (Charlotte, NC: Saint Benedict Press Classics, 2007)

The Man Nearest to Christ, Fr. Francis L. Filas, SJ (Milwaukee: Bruce Publishing Co., 1944)

St. Joseph and Daily Christian Living, Fr. Francis L. Filas, SJ (New York: The Macmillan Co., 1959)

"Miracle or a Wonder of Construction?" by Carl R. Albach, *Consulting Engineer* magazine, December 1965

"The Inexplicable Stairs," by Sr. M. Florian, OSF, *St. Joseph* magazine, April 1960

The Truth of Christmas Beyond the Myths: *The Gospels of the Infancy of Christ,* Fr. René Laurentin (Petersham, MA: St. Bede's Publications, May 1986)

Joseph of Nazareth, Fr. Federico Suárez (New York: Scepter Publishers, Inc., 1984, 2004)

Redemptoris Custos, "Guardian of the Redeemer," apostolic exhortation, John Paul II, August 15, 1989

PRAYERS TO ST. JOSEPH

Prayer to St. Joseph (to be said after the Rosary)
(by Pope Leo XIII)

To you, O Blessed Joseph, we come in our trials, and having asked the help of your most holy spouse, we confidently ask for your patronage. Through that sacred bond of charity that united you to the Immaculate Virgin Mother of God and through the fatherly love with which you embraced the Child Jesus, we humbly beg you to look graciously upon the beloved inheritance Jesus Christ purchased by His blood, and to aid us in our necessities with your power and strength.

O most provident guardian of the Holy Family, defend the chosen children of Jesus Christ. Most beloved father, dispel the evil of falsehood and sin. Our most mighty protector, graciously assist us from heaven in our struggle with the powers of darkness. And just as you once saved the Child Jesus from mortal danger, so now defend God's Holy Church from the snares of her enemies and from all adversity. Shield each one of us by your constant protection, so that, supported by your example and your help, we may live a virtuous life, die a holy death, and obtain eternal happiness in heaven. Amen.

Prayer to St. Joseph

O St. Joseph, whose protection is so great, so strong, so prompt before the throne of God, I place in you all my interests and desires. Do assist me by your powerful intercession and obtain for me from your Divine Son all spiritual blessings through Jesus Christ, Our Lord, so that having engaged here below your heavenly power, I may offer my thanksgiving and homage to the most loving of Fathers. O St. Joseph, I never weary contemplating you and Jesus asleep in your arms. I dare not approach while He reposes near your heart. Press Him in my name, kiss His fine head for me, and ask Him to return the kiss when I draw my dying breath. St. Joseph, patron of departing souls, pray for us. Amen.

(Those who read or carry this prayer will never die a sudden death, be drowned, effected by poison, burned in any fire, fall into enemy hands, or defeated in battle.)

Memorare to St. Joseph

Remember, O most chaste spouse of the Virgin Mary, that never was it known that anyone who implored your help and sought your intercession was left unaided. Full of confidence in your power, I fly unto you, and beg your protection. Despise not, O foster father of the Redeemer, my humble petition, but in your goodness, hear and answer me. Amen.

Litany of St. Joseph

Lord, have mercy on us.
Christ, have mercy on us.
Lord, have mercy on us.
Christ, hear us. Christ, graciously hear us.
God the Father of heaven,   *Have mercy on us.*
God the Son, Redeemer of the world,   "   "
God the Holy Spirit,   "   "
Holy Trinity, One God,   "   "

Response is "pray for us"
Holy Mary, pray for us,
St. Joseph,
Illustrious son of David,
Light of the patriarchs,
Spouse of the Mother of God,
Chaste guardian of the Virgin,
Foster-father of the Son of God,
Watchful defender of Christ,

Head of the Holy Family,
Joseph, most just,
Joseph, most chaste,
Joseph, most prudent,
Joseph, most valiant,
Joseph, most obedient,
Joseph, most faithful,
Mirror of patience,
Lover of poverty,
Model of workmen,
Glory of domestic life,
Guardian of virgins,
Pillar of families,
Solace of the afflicted,
Hope of the sick,
Patron of the dying,
Terror of demons,
Protector of God's Holy Church,
Lamb of God, You Who take away the sins of
   the world, spare us, O Lord.
Lamb of God, You Who take away the sins of
   the world, graciously hear us, O Lord.
Lamb of God, You Who take away the sins of
   the world, have mercy on us.

V. He made him lord of His house,
R. *And prince of all His possessions.*
V. Let us pray: O God, Who in Your marvelous
providence has deigned to choose St. Joseph to

be the spouse of Your most holy mother, grant, we beseech You, that we may deserve to have him for our intercessor in Heaven whom on earth we venerate as our protector, You Who live and reign forever and ever. Amen.

Novena Prayer to St. Joseph to Obtain a Special Favor

O Blessed St. Joseph, tenderhearted father, faithful guardian of Jesus, chaste spouse of the mother of God, I pray and beseech you to offer to God the Father His divine Son, bathed in blood on the Cross for sinners, and through the thrice holy Name of Jesus, obtain for us of the eternal Father the favor we implore. Appease the divine anger so justly inflamed by our crimes. Beg of Jesus mercy for your children. Amid the splendors of eternity, forget not the sorrows of those who suffer, those who pray, those who weep. May your prayers and those of your most holy spouse move the Heart of Jesus to pity and pardon and thus stay the almighty arm that smites us. Amen.

Prayer of Laborers
(by Pope St. Pius X)

O glorious St. Joseph, model of all who are devoted to labor, obtain for me the grace to work in the spirit of penance and in expiation of my many sins; to work conscientiously by placing love of duty above my inclinations; to gratefully and joyously deem it an honor to employ and to develop by labor the gifts I have received from God, to work methodically, peacefully, and in moderation and patience, without ever shrinking from it through weariness or difficulty of work. Above all, help me to work with purity of intention and unselfishness, having unceasingly before my eyes death and the account I have to render of time lost, talents unused, good not done, and vain complacency in success, so baneful to the work of God. All for Jesus, all for Mary, all to imitate thee, O Patriarch St. Joseph! This shall be my motto for life and eternity. Amen.

Prayer to St. Joseph the Worker
(by Bl. John XXIII)

O St. Joseph, guardian of Jesus, chaste spouse of Mary, you who passed your life in the perfect fulfillment of duty, sustaining the Holy Family of Nazareth with the work of your hands, kindly keep those who with total trust now come to you. You know their aspirations, their miseries, and their hopes. They come to you because they know that you understand and protect them. You, too, have known trial, toil, and weariness. But even in the midst of worries about the material life, your soul was filled with profound peace, and it exulted in unerring joy through intimacy with the Son of God Who was entrusted to you, and with Mary, His most sweet mother. May those whom you protect understand they are not alone in their toil, but show them how to discover Jesus at their side, to receive Him with grace, to guard Him faithfully, as you have done. And with your prayers obtain that in every family, in every factory, in every workshop, wherever a Christian works, all may be satisfied in charity, in patience, in justice, in seeking righteousness, so that abundant gifts may shower upon them from heaven.[1]

Prayer to St. Joseph before Mass & Holy Communion (from the Roman Missal)

Happy and blessed art thou, O Joseph, to whom it was given not only to see and to hear that God whom many kings desired to see, and saw not, to hear, and heard not; but also to hold Him in thine arms, to embrace Him, to clothe Him, and to guard and defend Him.

Pray for us, O blessed Joseph, that we may be made worthy of the promises of Christ.

Let us pray: O God, who hast given unto us a royal priesthood, vouchsafe, we beseech Thee, that as Blessed Joseph was found worthy to touch

with his hands and bear within his arms Thine
Only-begotten Son, born of the Virgin Mary,
so may we be made fit, by cleanness of heart and
purity of work, to serve at Thy holy altars; that
we may worthily receive the Most Sacred Body
and Blood of Thy Son now in this present world;
and deserve to attain an everlasting reward in
the world to come. Through the same Christ
our Lord. Amen.

Prayer to Obtain a Conversion

O glorious patriarch St. Joseph, who merited
to be called "just" by the Holy Spirit, I urgently
recommend to you the soul of (Name), which
Jesus redeemed at the price of His Precious
Blood.

You know how deplorable is the state
and how unhappy the life of those who have
banished this loving Savior from their hearts,
and how greatly they are exposed to the danger
of losing Him eternally. Permit not, I beseech
you, that a soul so dear to me should continue
any longer in its evil ways; preserve it from the
danger that threatens it; touch the heart of the
prodigal child and conduct him/her back to the
bosom of the fondest of fathers. Abandon him/
her not, I implore you, till you have opened to
him/her the gates of the Heavenly city, where
he/she will praise and bless you throughout

eternity for the happiness he/she will owe to your powerful intercession. Amen.

Prayer to St. Joseph for Purity

O Guardian of Virgins and holy Father St. Joseph, into whose faithful keeping were entrusted Christ Jesus, Innocence itself, and Mary, Virgin of virgins, I pray and beseech you by these dear pledges, Jesus and Mary, that, being preserved from all uncleanness, I may with spotless mind, pure heart and chaste body, ever serve Jesus and Mary most chastely all the days of my life. Amen.

Grant us, dear Joseph, to run life's pathway in an innocent fashion. May we be ever safe under your blest patronage.

O St. Joseph, foster father of our Lord Jesus Christ and true spouse of Mary the Virgin, pray for us.

Fr. Gilsdorf had a simple personal prayer he said many times each day:

Guardian of Jesus, Guardian of Mary, Guardian of the Church: Be my Guardian!

APPENDIX 3

Homily of Pope Benedict XVI
for the Feast of St. Joseph
Amadou Ahidjo Stadium of Yaoundé, Cameroon
Thursday, 19 March 2009

Dear Brother Bishops,
Dear Brothers and Sisters,

Praised be Jesus Christ Who has gathered us in this stadium today that we may enter more deeply into His life!

Jesus Christ brings us together on this day when the Church, here in Cameroon and throughout the world, celebrates the Feast of St. Joseph, husband of the Virgin Mary. I begin by wishing a very happy feast day to all those who, like myself, have received the grace of bearing this beautiful name, and I ask St. Joseph to grant them his special protection in guiding them toward the Lord Jesus Christ all the days of their life.

I also extend cordial best wishes to all the parishes, schools, colleges, and institutions named after St. Joseph. I thank Archbishop

Tonyé-Bakot of Yaoundé for his kind words,
and I warmly greet the representatives of the
African Episcopal Conferences who have
come to Yaoundé for the promulgation of the
Instrumentum Laboris of the Second Special
Assembly for Africa of the Synod of Bishops.

How can we enter into the specific grace
of this day? In a little while, at the end of Mass,
the liturgy will remind us of the focal point of
our meditation when it has us pray, "Lord, today
You nourish us at this altar as we celebrate the
feast of St. Joseph. Protect Your Church always,
and in Your love watch over the gifts You have
given us." We are asking the Lord to protect the
Church always—and He does!—just as Joseph
protected his family and kept watch over the
Child Jesus during His early years.

Our Gospel reading recalls this for us. The
angel said to Joseph, "Do not be afraid to take
Mary your wife into your home" (Matt 1:20),
and that is precisely what he did: "He did as the
angel of the Lord had commanded him" (Matt
1:24). Why was St. Matthew so keen to note
Joseph's trust in the words received from the
messenger of God, if not to invite us to imitate
this same loving trust?

Although the first reading we have just
heard does not speak explicitly of St. Joseph,
it does teach us a good deal about him. The

prophet Nathan, in obedience to God's command, tells David, "I will raise up your heir after you, sprung from your loins" (2 Sam 7:12). David must accept that he will die before seeing the fulfillment of this promise, which will come to pass "when (his) time comes" and he will rest "with (his) ancestors." We thus come to realize that one of mankind's most cherished desires—seeing the fruits of one's labors—is not always granted by God. I think of those among you who are mothers and fathers of families. Parents quite rightly desire to give the best of themselves to their children, and they want to see them achieve success. Yet make no mistake about what this "success" entails: What God asks David to do is to place his trust in Him. David himself will not see his heir who will have a throne "firm for ever" (2 Sam 7:16), for this heir, announced under the veil of prophecy, is Jesus. David puts his trust in God.

In the same way, Joseph trusts God when he hears His messenger the angel say to him, "Joseph, son of David, do not be afraid to take Mary your wife into your home. For it is through the Holy Spirit that this child has been conceived in her" (Matt 1:20). Throughout all of history, Joseph is the man who gives God the greatest display of trust, even in the face of such astonishing news.

Dear fathers and mothers here today, do you have trust in God Who has called you to be the fathers and mothers of His adopted children? Do you accept that He is counting on you to pass on to your children the human and spiritual values that you yourselves have received and that will prepare them to live with love and respect for His Holy Name? At a time when so many people have no qualms about trying to impose the tyranny of materialism, with scant concern for the most deprived, you must be very careful. Africa in general, and Cameroon in particular, place themselves at risk if they do not recognize the True Author of Life! Brothers and sisters … you who have received from God so many human virtues, take care of your souls! Do not let yourselves be captivated by selfish illusions and false ideals! Believe—yes!—continue to believe in God—Father, Son, and Holy Spirit—He alone truly loves you in the way you yearn to be loved, He alone can satisfy you, can bring stability to your lives. Only Christ is the way of Life.

God alone could grant Joseph the strength to trust the angel. God alone will give you, dear married couples, the strength to raise your family as He wants. Ask it of Him! God loves to be asked for what He wishes to give. Ask Him for the grace of a true and ever more faithful love patterned after His own. As the Psalm magnificently puts it: His "love is established for ever, His loyalty will stand as long as the heavens" (Ps 88:3).

Just as on other continents, the family today—in your country and across Africa—is experiencing a difficult time; but fidelity to God will help see it through. Certain values of the traditional life have been overturned. Relationships between different generations have evolved in a way that no longer favors the transmission of accumulated knowledge and inherited wisdom. Too often we witness a rural exodus not unlike that known in many other periods of human history. The quality of family ties is deeply affected by this. Uprooted and fragile members of the younger generation who often—sadly—are without gainful employment, seek to cure their pain by living in ephemeral and man-made paradises which we know will never guarantee the human being a deep, abiding happiness. Sometimes the African people too are constrained to flee from themselves and abandon everything that once made up their interior richness. Confronted with the phenomenon of rapid urbanization, they leave the land, physically and morally: not as Abraham had done in response to the Lord's call, but as a kind of interior exile that alienates them from their very being, from their brothers and sisters, and from God Himself.

Is this an irreversible, inevitable development? By no means! More than ever, we must "hope against all hope" (Rom 4:18). Here I wish to acknowledge with appreciation and gratitude the remarkable work done by countless associations that promote the life of faith and the practice of charity. May they be warmly thanked! May they find in the word of God renewed strength to carry out their projects for the integral development of the human person in Africa, especially in Cameroon!

The first priority will consist in restoring a sense of the acceptance of life as a gift from God. According to both sacred Scripture and the wisest traditions of your continent, the arrival of a child is always a gift, a blessing from God. Today it is high time to place greater emphasis on this: Every human being, every tiny human person, however weak, is created "in the image and likeness of God" (Gen 1:27). Every person must live! Death must not prevail over life! Death will never have the last word!

Sons and daughters of Africa, do not be afraid to believe, to hope, and to love; do not be afraid to say that Jesus is the Way, the Truth, and the Life, and that we can be saved by Him alone. St. Paul is indeed an inspired author given to the Church by the Holy Spirit as a "teacher of nations" (1 Tim 2:7) when he tells us that

Abraham, "hoping against hope, believed that he should become the father of many nations; as he had been told, 'So shall your descendants be'" (Rom 4:18).

"Hoping against hope:" Is this not a magnificent description of a Christian? Africa is called to hope through you and in you! With Jesus Christ, who trod the African soil, Africa can become the continent of hope! We are all members of the peoples that God gave to Abraham as his descendants. Each and every one of us was thought, willed, and loved by God. Each and every one of us has a role to play in the plan of God: Father, Son, and Holy Spirit. If discouragement overwhelms you, think of the faith of Joseph; if anxiety has its grip on you, think of the hope of Joseph, that descendant of Abraham who hoped against hope; if exasperation or hatred seizes you, think of the love of Joseph, who was the first man to set eyes on the human face of God in the person of the Infant conceived by the Holy Spirit in the womb of the Virgin Mary. Let us praise and thank Christ for having drawn so close to us, and for giving us Joseph as an example and model of love for Him.

Dear brothers and sisters, I want to say to you once more from the bottom of my heart: Like Joseph, do not be afraid to take Mary into your home. That is to say, do not be afraid to love the Church. Mary, Mother of the Church, will teach you to follow your pastors, to love your bishops, your priests, your deacons, and your catechists; to heed what they teach you and to pray for their intentions. Husbands, look upon the love of Joseph for Mary and Jesus; those preparing for marriage, treat your future spouse as Joseph did; those of you who have given yourselves to God in celibacy, reflect upon the teaching of the Church, our Mother: "Virginity or celibacy for the sake of the Kingdom of God not only does not contradict the dignity of marriage but presupposes and confirms it. Marriage and virginity are two ways of expressing and living the one mystery of the Covenant of God with His people" (*Redemptoris Custos*, 20).

Once more, I wish to extend a particular word of encouragement to fathers so that they may take St. Joseph as their model. He who kept watch over the Son of Man is able to teach them the deepest meaning of their own fatherhood. In the same way, each father receives his children from God, and they are created in God's own image and likeness. St. Joseph was the spouse of Mary. In the same way, each father sees himself entrusted with the mystery of womanhood through his own wife. Dear fathers, like St. Joseph, respect and love your spouse; and by your love and your wise presence, lead your children to God where they must be (cf. Luke 2:49).

Finally, to all the young people present, I offer words of friendship and encouragement: As you face the challenges of life, take courage! Your life is priceless in the eyes of God! Let Christ take hold of you, agree to pledge your love to Him, and—why not?—maybe even do so in the priesthood or in the consecrated life! This is the supreme service. To the children who no longer have a father or who live abandoned in the poverty of the streets, to those forcibly separated from their parents, to the maltreated and abused, to those constrained to join paramilitary forces that are terrorizing some countries, I would like to say: God loves you, He has not forgotten you, and St. Joseph protects you! Invoke him with confidence.

May God bless you and watch over you! May He give you the grace to keep advancing toward Him with fidelity! May He give stability to your lives so that you may reap the fruits He awaits from you! May He make you witnesses of His love here in Cameroon and to the ends of the earth! I fervently beg Him to give you a taste of the joy of belonging to Him, now and forever. Amen.

ENDNOTES

Chapter One

1. Matt 1:19
2. Ps 105[104]:21
3. Gen 41:55
4. *Quemadmodum Deus* (QD), decree, Sacred Congregation of Rites, December 8, 1870.
5. *Quamquam Pluries* (QP), "On Devotion to St. Joseph," encyclical, Pope Leo XIII, no. 4, August 15, 1889
6. John 6:51

Chapter Two

1. Luke 3:23–24
2. Matt 1:16
3. *The Truth of Christmas Beyond the Myths: The Gospels of the Infancy of Christ*, Fr. René Laurentin, pp. 334-335 (Petersham, MA: St Bede's Publication; May 1986)
4. *Sermo* 51, No. 16ff
5. Deut 25:5
6. *The Truth of Christmas Beyond the Myths: The Gospels of the Infancy of Christ*, p. 355
7. Ibid.
8. Luke 1:27
9. Matt 13:55
10. *Dialogue with Tryphon*, no. 88

Chapter Three

1. Cf. Luke 1:26
2. Is 11:1–2

3 Num 17:1, 5, 6
4 Matt 1:18–19
5 *St. Joseph and Daily Christian Living*, p. 62, Fr. Francis L. Filas, SJ (New York: The Macmillan Co., 1959)
6 cf. John 8
7 *Opus Imperfectum in Matthaeum*, hom. 1
8 *Opera Omnia*, Vol. 19, *De Mysteriis Vitae Christi*, Q. 29, Disp. 7, sec. 2, nos. 5–6.
9 *St. Joseph and Daily Christian Living*, p. 62
10 *In Matthaeum*, 1, 2
11 *St. Joseph and Daily Christian Living*, p. 62

Chapter Four

1 Matt 1:20
2 Cf. Gen 22:1–14
3 Matt 1:24
4 Matt 1:20
5 Father gives no cite for this text. The two most likely sources for it are *Sermo 51*, no. 21; ML 38, 344–345 or *De nuptiis et concupiscentia*, bk. 1. c. 11; ML 44, 420–421
6 Letter of Ignatius of Antioch to the Ephesians 19:1 (for the full text of the letter, see *Ignatius of Antioch: A New Translation and Theological Commentary*, Dr. Kenneth J. Howell, p. 70 (Zanesville, OH: Coming Home Resources, 2009). See also Origen, *Homilies on Luke*, 6, 3-4.
7 *Summa Theologica* III, Q. 29, Art. 1 and 2, *Catena Aurea in Matthaeum*, cap. 1, *lectio* 9
8 *Homilia II super Missus Est* 12, 13 passim.
9 *Summa Theologica* III, Q. 29, Art. 1
10 Matt 1:25
11 Ps 109:1 as cited by St. Paul in 1 Cor 15:25
12 2 Kings 6:23
13 *Adversus Helvidium*, 6
14 Op. cit, 19
15 *Sermo 51*, No. 26, 30.
16 *Opusculum 17 de coelibatu sacerdotum*, cap 3
17 *In Matthaeum*, 1, 19

Chapter Five

1   Luke 2:4–5
2   Matt 13:55
3   Mic 5:2 as cited in Matt 2:6
4   Luke 2:7
5   John 1:11
6   John 1:12
7   Cf. Ps 105:21

Chapter Six

1   Luke 2:21
2   Cf. Luke 2:22–23, 28, 39
3   *St. Joseph and Daily Christian Living*, p. 89
4   Cf. Luke 1:62–63
5   Luke 3:23
6   Matt 23:11, Luke 14:8–11; cf. Luke 1:46–55
7   *St. Joseph and Daily Christian Living*, p. 80
8   *Ibid.*, p. 81
9   *Catechesis VII de patre*, No. 9
10 Eph 3:14, 15
11 Luke 2:41–51
12 *Our Father's Plan: God's Arrangements and Our Responses*,
    by Fr. William G. Most (Manassas, VA: Trinity
    Communications, 1988), reviewed in Fr. Gilsdorf's other
    book, *The Signs of the Times: Understanding the Church since
    Vatican II*, pp. 333–335.
13 Matt 2:16
14 Matt 2:11
15 Matt 2:13–14
16 Luke 2:19
17 Luke 2:51

Chapter Seven

1   Cf., *QP*, nos. 3, 4
2   Gen 3:19
3   *The Man Nearest to Christ*, Fr. Francis L. Filas, SJ, pp. 58-59
    (Milwaukee: Bruce Publishing Co., 1944)

⁴ *Bonum sane (BonS)* (On the occasion of the Fiftieth anniversary of the title of Joseph's universal patronage) motu proprio, Benedict XV, July 25, 1920. See *Acta Apostolicae Sedis (AAS)*, 12, 313 (1920). As Fr. Blaine Burkey, OFM Cap, notes, Benedict also "sanctioned a proper preface in Joseph's honor and added his invocation to the Divine Praises."

⁵ Cf. Luke 10:23

⁶ *Neminem Fugit (NF)*, "Everyone Knows," apostolic brief, Leo XIII, June 14, 1892

⁷ *Ibid.*

⁸ "Radio Message to Catholic School Students in the United States of America," Pius XII, February 19, 1958: AAS 50 (1958), p. 174

⁹ John Paul II, General Audience address, December 30, 1988

¹⁰ *Fulgens Corona*, "Proclaiming a Marian Year," encyclical, Pius XII, no. 10, September 8, 1953

¹¹ Matt 11:11; Luke 7:28

¹² "The Cultus of the Heart of St. Joseph: An Inquiry into the *Status Quæstionis*," by Msgr. Arthur Burton Calkins, 9° Symposium international de Joséphologie, à Kevelaer du 25.09 au 2.10.2005. The article discusses the June 14, 1873, prohibition on page 5: "The first negative intervention on the part of the Holy See, which is presently available, is the response of the Sacred Congregation of Rites to the Bishop of Nantes who had asked whether the invocation *Cor Sancti Joseph purissimum, ora pro nobis* could be used in non-liturgical functions. On 14 June 1873 the Sacred Congregation ordered its Secretary to write to the Bishop of Nantes warning him that the cultus of the Heart of St. Joseph is not approved by the Holy See" [*Monendum esse per epistolam Rmum. Dominum Episcopum cultum Cordis S. Iosephi non esse ab Apostolica Sede approbatum*].<Footnote 17: Blaine Burkey, OFM Cap, *Pontificia Josephina* C558 [197–198] in *Cahiers de Joséphologie* 12 (1964) 377–378>. Msgr. Calkins' article can be read at http://www.josephologie. info/documents/reportages/symp-Mgr-Calkins.pdf.

Chapter Eight

[1]   Luke 19:37–42
[2]   *QD*
[3]   *NF*
[4]   *BonS*
[5]   *Divini Redemptoris*, "On Atheistic Communism," encyclical,
      Pope Pius XI, no. 81, March 19, 1937. As previously noted,
      this act of Pius XI's was followed by the allied feast of St.
      Joseph the Worker by Pius XII in 1955. Both of these acts
      were sequels to the title, "Patron of Workers."

Chapter Nine

[1]   As quoted in *The Man Nearest to Christ*, p. 104
[2]   *Ibid.*, p. 100
[3]   From *The Autobiography of St. Teresa*, Chapter 6
[4]   Cf. articles by Sister M. Florian, OSF, and Carl R. Albach,
      as listed in "Suggested readings"
[5]   *Brother André: The Wonder Man of Mount Royal*, by Henri-
      Paul Bergeron, CSC, translated by Real Boudreau, CSC
      (Montreal: Fides Publishers, 1958)
[6]   *The Man Nearest to Christ*, p. 109
[7]   John 21:25

Appendix 2

[1]   From the message broadcast to workers, Sunday, May 1,
      1960, cf., *Discorsi, messaggi, colloqui, cit.*, vol. II, p. 326. [Ital.:
      AAS LII, 400]

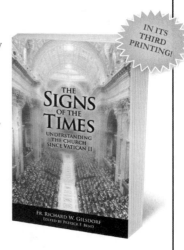

To order more copies for:

- Your pastor
- Your deacon
- Your director of Religious Education
- Your book club
- Your library
- A seminarian
- Your bishop
- Your bookstore
- A cherished friend or loved one
- Anyone!

Ask us about bulk discounts.

W5180 Jefferson St.
Necedah, WI 54646
Phone: 800-932-3826
Fax: 608-565-2025
www.CatholicWord.com

Catholic resources for kids, teens & adults
Books, Music, Studies

NOTES

NOTES

NOTES

NOTES